Dimitri Tiomkin

Dimitri Tiomkin
A Portrait

by
Christopher Palmer

T. E. BOOKS

Acknowledgements

Illustration 29, courtesy of RKO General Pictures.
Illustration 15, courtesy of and © Academy of Motion Pictures
Illustration 21, photo by Jenkins for Columbia Pictures
Illustration 7 colour, courtesy of Columbia Pictures Industries Inc
Illustration 33, music from 'Gunfight at OK Corral',
copyright © 1956 by Paramount Pictures Corporation,
Hal B. Wallis and Joseph H. Hazen. All rights reserved.
Front Cover illustration: portrait by Gyenes, Madrid
Illustration 24, from the United Artists release 'The Alamo'
© 1960 The Alamo Company
Illustrations 17 and 11, courtesy of MGM/UA Entertainment Co.,
Illustrations 4 colour, 30, 31, 32, 38, 41, © Warner Bros, inc.

First published 1984 by T.E. Books
3 Stanley Crescent, London W.11

© 1984 Olivia Tiomkin

ISBN 0 9509439 0 8

Production in association with Book Production
Consultants, Cambridge and The Levison Company, London

Typeset by Multiplex

Printed in Great Britain at the University Press, Cambridge

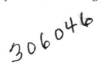

Contents

List of illustrations   *Page* 8

Part I   Chronology   13

Part II   Perspective   61

Part III   Landmarks   77

                 Principal Awards and Honours   134

                 Complete Filmography   136

                 Index   141

List of Illustrations

Frontispiece: Dimitri Tiomkin. Painting by Grimman 1928

		Pages
1	With his mother	12
2	Aged 5	15
3	Aged about 17	21
4	With 2 fellow students	23
5	In Berlin early 1920s	26
6	Paris concert 1924	29
7	With Albertina, late 1920's	32
8	Carnegie Hall recital 1927	34
9	Paris handbill 1928	37
10	Gershwin dedication 1928	39
11	Arthur Lange conducting one of Tiomkin's early MGM compositions	40
12	With Capra, Columbia Musical Director Morris Stoloff, Max Steiner, recording *Lost Horizon*	43
13	Tiomkin's conducting debut at the Hollywood Bowl, 16 August 1938	46
14	Tex Ritter – *High Noon*	50
15	With Alfred Newman, Ned Washington and Walt Disney, two Oscars for *High Noon*	51
16	The Composer's name on the marquee.	52
17	With William Wyler, Gary Cooper, and Jester Hairston *Friendly Persuasion*	54
18	Outside the Kremlin, 1966 – *Tchaikovsky*	55

19	With Leopold Stokowski, 1972	56
20	With Olivia	57
21	With Henry Eichheim	79
22	Capra, Ronald Colman and Tiomkin – *Lost Horizon*	81
23	Jennifer Jones and Gregory Peck on screen. Recording *Duel in the Sun*	85
24	Scene from *The Alamo*	89
25	With Mr and Mrs John Wayne – London premiere of *The Alamo* 1960	90
26	With Tex Ritter – recording *High Noon*	93
27	Sketch for the *High Noon* theme-song	94
28	Hitchcock dedication	97
29	With Howard Hawks	100
30	*Land of the Pharaohs* recording	102
31	With George Stevens and Chill Wills – *Giant*	103
32	With Edna Ferber	104
33	Score (End Title) of *Gunfight at the OK Corral*	106
34	Conducting Pittsburgh Symphony Orchestra – *Rhapsody of Steel*	109
35	Scene from *Rhapsody of Steel*	110
36	Recording *Search for Paradise:* the Himalayas on the Cinerama Screen	112
37	With Robert Merrill – *Search for Paradise*	115
38	Spencer Tracy – *The Old Man and the Sea*	118
39	Composition sketch – *Guns of Navarone*	120
40	Recording *Fall of the Roman Empire*	123/124
41	With Nicholas Ray on the set of *55 Days at Peking*	126

Colour Plates

		Opposite Page
1	Duel in the Sun – *album cover*	64
2	Rio Bravo – *sheet music montage*	65

Opposite Page

3	'I Confess', *sheet music montage*	80
4	Giant – *poster*	81
5	Rhapsody of Steel – *poster*	96
6	Search for Paradise – *album cover*	97
7	Guns of Navarone – *album cover*	112
8	Tchaikovsky – *album cover*	113

Front cover: Portrait by Gyenes, Madrid

Back cover: Recording *Tchaikovsky*, Mosfilm Studios, 1968

PART I

With his mother

Chronology

Dimitri Tiomkin was born on 10 May 1894 in the Ukraine. His father was a distinguished pathologist and an associate of Professor Ehrlich, the inventor of 606, the Salvarsan cure for syphilis. His mother, remembered by Tiomkin as 'small, blonde, merry and vivacious' was herself a musician and wanted the young Dimitri to be a pianist. She started to teach him the piano as soon as it was physically practicable.

At the age of seven the boy was brought by his father to St Petersburg and placed in a children's piano class. The pre-Revolutionary St Petersburg impressed the young Tiomkin as 'a city of splendour and strangeness'. The Ukraine was to feature in his memory, as he put it, 'only distantly and dreamily'. He would remember the brightness of the stars in the black night sky, a sight repeated in his experience only in the Mexican desert. And he would remember the peasant women laundering their clothes in the river, singing the old, sad songs as they beat the clothes rhythmically with sticks.

Tiomkin lodged with a family whose son was on the staff of the St Petersburg Conservatoire, teaching the piano to first-study violinists such as Zimbalist, Elman and Heifetz. Dimitri entered Professor Winkler's class and was promptly forbidden to study anything except scales and a solitary Haydn sonata. His dreary practice was occasionally interrupted and enlivened by a skinny, freckled boy, all arms and legs, pulling faces and thumbing his nose at the miserable Dimitri. It was Sergei Prokofiev, no respecter of persons or convention even at that early age. Not surprisingly, Dimitri was soon bored by his studies and began to spend more of his time on the banks of the Neva than in the small studio at the Conservatoire.

Tiomkin's father left the Ukraine and went to Berlin to work as a doctor attached to the Russian Embassy. Through mischance or oversight, the money he sent for Dimitri's board and lodging ceased to arrive. The family set the child to work in a local bakery making priojki, a sort of meat pie. Tiomkin soon wrote to his mother about the Dickensian conditions he was now suffering. Furiously she descended on St Petersburg and whisked her son away back to the Ukraine. Almost immediately she moved the family back to St Petersburg and set up home in the suburbs. She realized that Dimitri's enthusiasm for the piano had not survived Professor Winkler's somewhat unimaginative teaching and the boy was sent to a conventional school for the next four years to continue his formal education. He was later to be grateful for this more broadly-based education than he might otherwise have had. The emphasis of the school's curriculum was on literature and Russian history and Dimitri also learned French and German, both of which were to stand him in good stead in future years, and mathematics for which, not unlike many other musicians, he showed a pronounced gift. Gradually his interest in music reasserted itself and he found himself not only practising pieces for school concerts, but also writing small piano works of his own. His mother was naturally delighted by this turn of events and, by the time Dimitri was thirteen, he was eager for her to arrange for him to take the entrance examinations for the Conservatoire.

After a daunting series of tests and interviews with solemn and elderly professors, Dimitri was ushered into the presence of the Director, Alexander Glazunov. The colourful and eccentric composer was then at the height of his fame and was treated with great respect by St Petersburg society. He was a tremendous influence on many of his students, not least Tiomkin. He informed the boy that he had passed his entrance examination and then asked to hear something Tiomkin had composed himself. The latter played a short piece which he later recognized as sentimental and derivative of pieces he knew by Schumann. Glazunov not only accepted him as a piano student, allocating him to Felix Blumenfeld, who was incidentally Vladimir Horowitz's teacher, but also advised the boy to study composition, suggesting he join Glazunov's own class in harmony and counterpoint.

Tiomkin described Glazunov as 'a good-humoured Titan' and 'a huge seal in a frock-coat, with small eyes and a large flowing moustache'. He was a remarkable teacher, both severe and encouraging. Mikhail Gnessin defined Glazunov's basic emotion as a 'delight in an exquisitely arranged universe' and his teaching of harmony and counterpoint was marked by an almost obsessive insistence on the classical correctness of his student's exercises. His ear and memory were astounding: he could pinpoint to the bar a stray consecutive fifth and he had the rare trick of being able to reproduce complete a piece of up to symphonic length when he had heard it only once. He had perfect pitch. Despite

Aged 5

his teacher's reputation for icy precision, Tiomkin describes Glazunov's approach as romantic rather than intellectual: 'He had the intelligence of a scientist. He was a classicist in form, but a romantic in spirit, and his method was not severely scholastic. I think of his influence as that of a radiant personality.'

Glazunov had two major weaknesses: firstly for alcohol and secondly for his young female piano students. Shostakovich, who was a student of Glazunov's a few years after Tiomkin, became involved in providing the desperate Glazunov with state-controlled alcohol to which Shostakovich's father had access during the early years of the Revolution. Shostakovich also suspected that Glazunov had some secret contraption built into his desk at the Conservatoire, a tube of some kind through which he could siphon a constant stream of alcohol, apparently undetected. As evidence for this, Shostakovich cites Glazunov's permanently hunched position at his desk and his reluctance ever to take more than two or three steps away from it. His susceptibility to his female students was public knowledge and a public joke. The girl's actual ability, or more often lack of it, appeared to have very little effect on Glazunov's opinion of her. For the duration of his infatuation she would be, according to her smitten professor, the latest genius of the keyboard.

Although Glazunov, according to Shostakovich, lived quietly and peacefully at home with his overbearing, over-protective mother, feeding the fish in his enormous fishtank, and seeing the world only in terms of music, he also led a lively and busy social life. The Glazunov family owned the largest book-publishing firm in Russia and was consequently extremely rich. Alexander Glazunov's uncle was Mayor of St Petersburg and was famous for holding banquets so large that he needed to use a pair of binoculars in order to survey his distant guests. His nephew too loved entertaining in expensive restaurants, insisting on the best food, the best wine and the best company.

In the days before the Revolution, Glazunov had great influence in government circles, which he was willing to use on behalf of his students and on behalf of the Conservatoire. These were the days of the pogroms and the strongly anti-Semitic laws of the time serverely limited the rights of Russian Jews, even confining them to particular geographical areas. Glazunov constantly used his influence with the Ministry of the Interior to procure special permissions for his Jewish students to travel freely. Glazunov was firm and calm under pressure from the authorities, and when pressed to give details of the number of Jewish students at the Conservatoire, would reply only 'We don't keep count.'

For Shostakovich, Glazunov was 'a living legend' and he claimed that of the thousands of students graduating from the Conservatoire while Glazunov was Director there, 'it would be hard to name one who wasn't indebted to Glazunov in some way. He became a man blessed for his good deeds by every working musician in the country. He sacrificed everything for the Conservatoire — his time, his serenity, and finally his creativity.'

One way in which Glazunov was able to help his impoverished students was by arranging for them to teach the piano to the children of his wealthy, aristocratic friends. Glazunov's recommendation could open the door to that select, socialite world where employers were more inclined to boast of the families with whom they shared their piano teacher's service than to enquire about the quality of his teaching. Tiomkin would long remember the caviar and madeira set out for teacher and pupil and his tuition fee left discreetly on the piano in a scented envelope.

Tiomkin gave piano lessons to Glazunov's own niece and was soon supplementing the small amount of money his family could give him with income from piano lessons for the cream of St Petersburg society. Another source of income was playing the piano for silent films. Tiomkin tried hard to make the music fit the action on the screen and after one performance where a murder scene had inspired him to imitate the sounds of strangulation — something that had achieved instant popularity with the cinema audience — he became the sound effects man as well.

He also improvised accompaniments for the live performances of Max Linder, the inspired pantomime comedian. When Linder came to St Petersburg on tour just before the outbreak of the First World War, although he arrived in the city by train, he ordered a plane to fly him from the station to the Astoria Hotel, where he was staying. The spectacular arrival was certainly effective and it was perhaps one of the first occasions on which Tiomkin was to be aware of the relationship between a public image and the size and enthusiasm of a popular audience. For the rest of his life Tiomkin considered Linder one of the truly great comedians, on a par with Chaplin in his ability to manipulate the sympathies of an audience. Like many brilliant intuitive performers he was completely unpredictable on stage and it was all Tiomkin could do to keep pace with the lightning changes of mood and the frequent eruptions of entirely new material. But it was a challenge that Tiomkin relished and he learned much from the risk-taking, instinctive Linder who, none the less, had the most acute analytical understanding of his own performances.

These were pleasant times for the young Tiomkin and his friends. He and his fellow students were well enough off financially not to have to be constantly worried about money and they whole-heartedly subscribed to Glazunov's high artistic principles, believing that art was everything and that nothing mattered beyond the ideals of music.

Tiomkin describes a typical evening during this period of his life when, for the student and his girl, St Petersburg might take on an almost magical, idyllic quality: 'We would take a carriage, a droshky, for a drive along the ornate avenues. Spring had come and there was the fragrance of lilacs everywhere. The white nights had come, and we would drive along holding hands, perhaps, in the glowing mystery of almost endless evening when the sky was like a pearl spreading over St Petersburg. The white nights and the lilacs, it was all like a perfumed dream.'

The meeting place for Bohemian society in St Petersburg was the poets' night club, 'The Stray Dog', owned and run by Vera Provin, known to Tiomkin and his friends as 'The Owl', and her husband. 'The Stray Dog' was a converted cellar with its windows completely blocked up. The walls were covered by paintings, notably by Sergey Sudeykin. The Menu consisted of cheap Caucasian wine, vodka and sandwiches. The prices were variable and depended on the whim of Vera Provin. Her own appearance was imposing: she wore dramatic make-up, her hands were covered with rings and her arms with bracelets. She was a shrewd judge of artistic talent and had attracted around her a circle of painters, poets, musicians and dancers of outstanding creative ability.

The exotic clientele itself attracted the wealthy bourgeoisie who came to be entertained and amused by the excitable artistic community of 'The Stray Dog'. It was these customers, the 'pharmacists', who subsidized the artists who had made 'The Stray Dog' their home. The club came alive between midnight and dawn when all the latest avant-garde ideas were discussed and embraced. St Petersburg looked to Paris for inspiration and, at the time Tiomkin was frequenting 'The Stray Dog', the painters were embracing cubism; the writers, free verse; and the musicians, the then most controversial of modernists, Debussy.

Glazunov and the rest of the music staff at the Conservatoire disapproved of modernism in general and of Debussy in particular. Although Glazunov had been much influenced himself by Mussorgsky and Rimsky-Korsakov, he had turned back in later years to Josquin des Prés, Roland de Lassus, Palestrina and Giovanni Gabrieli, delighting in the clarity and purity of their music. Glazunov considered Debussy's music cloudy and neurotic, and he thought his innovations mere sensation-seeking.

Tiomkin began to lead a kind of artistic double-life, attracted equally by new and old, spending his days at the Conservatoire and his nights at 'The Stray Dog', where he had begun to play the piano as a way of settling his bills. Here he was open to influences from innovators in all art-forms. The Italian futurist Marinetti was expounding his ideas for 'symphonies of noise'; Meyerhold was developing in public his theories of drama, ballet and opera; and above all there was Mayakovsky, remembered by Tiomkin as 'the very opposite of the pale aesthete who writes verses... of a tall, powerful build, with a handsome face so rugged... it might have been carved with an axe. His manner was overbearing, his voice loud and arrogant, and he was always contradicting everyone and... forever inflicting his revolutionary political views on the pharmacists, threatening them with socialism in Russia and promising the obliteration of their whole class.'

Prokofiev was another familiar figure at 'The Stray Dog'. He was at this time the *enfant terrible* of the Conservatoire and his attitude to the world at large was provocative and iconoclastic. The impressionism of Debussy held no attraction for him, and his music was already full of what to his contemporaries sounded like wild energy, violent discord and abrasive aggression.

At the end of Tiomkin's second term at the Conservatoire, Glazunov asked him if he would like to spend the summer on the Princess Bariatinsky's country estate at Ivanoskoye Selo. The Princess was the daughter of Alexander II, the Tsar who had been responsible for freeing the serfs and who was later assassinated by the nihilists. The Princess required a young man to accompany her singing. Glazunov told Tiomkin he would be well paid and warned him to take his very best clothes, including the gold-trimmed uniform and dress sword that Conservatoire students were required to wear on formal occasions.

The princess Bariatinsky was a widow in her early thirties and had inherited the immense wealth of her husband's family. The estate, deep in south-central Russia, consisted of two fantastic, fairy-tale palaces, the one a copy of the Tsar's Winter Palace in St Petersburg and the other, dating from the time of the war with Persia, built in Moslem style with a dome and minarets. The Persian palace had been constructed solely to make the Imam, the prisoner of an earlier Bariatinksy, feel comfortably at home.

The Princess was beautiful, melancholy and lonely. She had spent much of her early life in Western Europe and spoke Russian with a

French accent. She had a naturally good singing voice, but it had not been properly trained. Her taste in music was sentimental and, as well as accompanying her as she sang through her repertoire of arias from *Tosca* and Neapolitan songs, Tiomkin was expected to play Chopin and Grieg to her. He also made some attempts to teach the Princess's two boisterous sons the piano, but without success.

Towards the end of Tiomkin's stay at Ivanoskoye Selo, news arrived of the outbreak of the First World War. The Princess decided to convert her family estate at Yalta in the Crimea into an army hospital for officers. She wanted to supervise the organization herself and she set out for St Petersburg to arrange matters with the military authorities there. Tiomkin too returned to St Petersburg — now renamed Petrograd — with instructions to visit the Princess and continue her musical tuition.

In many ways life in Petrograd was not greatly changed by the outbreak of war. There was, if anything, even more frivolity and conspicuous expenditure as the soldiery threw riotous parties and factory owners and war profiteers spent their newly acquired wealth. There were emotional scenes at the railway stations as the new recruits were parted from their families and there was a general air of suspicion and uneasiness. The people had expected, if war was declared, to be fighting against England and not Germany. There was very little public information explaining the reasons for war. Moreover, since the 1905 defeat in the Japanese war, there was little popular confidence in the competence of the Russian military leaders. Luckily for Tiomkin, the authorities were easily dissuaded from conscripting music students and Glazunov managed to protect many of his students from military service.

The outbreak of war brought Tiomkin's father back to Petrograd from Berlin along with the rest of the Embassy staff. His recently acquired habits of German precision and efficiency stood him in good stead when he came to be appointed as head of the Russian Red Cross hospitals. His return did not mean, however, that the family was to be reunited. Tiomkin's parents had long been estranged and were now legally separated. The father was not impressed by his untidy, artistic son and took no interest in Dimitri's progress at the Conservatoire, although he thoroughly approved of the influential social connection with Princess Bariatinsky. Relations between father and son were not improved by the discovery of an exchange of love letters between Dimitri and a young girl-friend. Burning the correspondence was an act not calculated to endear the returning father to his son.

Aged about 17

A further contact with the aristocracy that Tiomkin made through Glazunov was with Count Sheremetiev. Sheremetiev had an estate including a large lake near Moscow and he would pay an occasional visit to the Conservatoire where he was invariably received with great pomp and ceremony. As well as being an amateur fireman – he owned a fire company and loved riding to fires on a fire-engine, dressed up in a uniform and helmet, blowing on his bugle – Sheremetiev was a considerable amateur musician. From time to time he gave public concerts, conducting works that were not too musically demanding, and he was in fact responsible for introducing Sousa's marches to Russia.

Tiomkin was engaged by the Count to give music lessons to Miss Ruby, the Count's black mistress. She had been a singer in a negro minstrel show in her native New Orleans and had met the Count when the show was touring Russia. Miss Ruby could sing and play the piano only by ear and the sixteen-year-old Tiomkin was employed to teach her to read music. They used the sheet music from the old minstrel shows and this was the first time Tiomkin had come across American popular music and, in particular, ragtime. The use of syncopation fascinated him.

Another surprise encounter with American music came at 'The Stray Dog'. A parcel arrived from America wrapped in the pages of a New York theatrical magazine in which was printed the music of 'Alexander's Ragtime Band'. The tune was played continually at 'The Stray Dog' and a new dance was invented to fit the unfamiliar off-beat rhythms. The habitués of 'The Stray Dog' called it a Bear Dance and shuffled their feet and swung their shoulders in their own interpretation of the catchy song.

Tiomkin soon heard more news of the Princess Bariatinsky. While nursing her wounded officers at Yalta, she had fallen in love with one of them and for Prince Serge Obolensky's first visit to Ivanoskoye Selo the Princess wanted Tiomkin to provide the piano music. Tiomkin described the magnificent reception with which the Princess greeted her guest: 'Obolensky arrived on a night train, and when the carriage brought him down the long avenue to the twin palaces, it rolled between two lines of peasants holding aloft flaming torches of pine. It was a scene from the time of Catherine the Great.'

In Obolensky the Princess's two practical-joke-playing sons found a kindred spirit. Obolensky remembered Tiomkin as frail-looking, nervous and extraordinarily shy, and the two did not become friends until much

With two fellow students

later when Obolensky and the two boys stuffed Tiomkin's bed full of horse brushes from the stable. Luckily Tiomkin was able to take it in good part and his shock and outrage soon turned to laughter. The ice was broken. Obolensky and the Princess soon married and whenever they were in Petrograd Tiomkin was expected to visit them and to play the piano for them.

As the Great War continued, the social and educational divisions of Tsarist Russia became more apparent. The nihilists and the Marxists gained in strength. The news from the front was bad and many agreed with Rasputin in his call for Russia to make peace with Germany. The scene was being set for the Revolution.

Tiomkin describes the curious innocence of the middle-class intelligentsia of the time: 'We were an example of how people can be unaware of the approach of a cataclysm, then ignorant of what is happening, and finally mistaken about what has happened. By "we" I mean the people I knew as a Conservatoire student: fellow students and professors and their circles, bohemian artists and intelligentsia, the families of my pupils, some aristocrats but mostly middle class. It was a world apart from workers, peasants, soldiers, and revolutionary agitators. They too, no doubt, were taken by surprise by the social eruption; but we lived in a special kind of illusion. We knew the history of revolutionary movements in Russia. We knew things were going badly in the war, that there were corruption and defeatism on the home front. We talked of the danger of a revolution, but we had no feeling that it could happen now.'

In February 1917, Tsar Nicholas II abdicated and a republic was declared. At first, there was no real difference in the day-to-day life of the people. There was general enthusiasm for the liberal government of Kerensky and its new ideas of freedom, democracy and patriotism. Tiomkin, with a group of friends, was inspired by the new commitment to the war and volunteered for active service. He found himself assigned to a group entertaining the troops. He toured with the ballerina Karsavina and also spent some time in the Arctic port of Murmansk.

The October Revolution put an end to the democracy and free debate of the previous few months. However, it was Bolshevist policy to preserve existing cultural institutions and the Conservatoire remained untouched, with Glazunov, now somewhat anachronistic in his formal frockcoat, still as its Director.

The food shortages became much worse as the railway system broke down. Whole meals were concocted of potato peelings and weeds. The black market prospered. Money was now useless and barter was the order of the day. Jewellery and silverware were used to buy a sack of beans or a loaf of bread. Tiomkin still managed to give some piano lessons, but now he was paid in potatoes or sausages, and the madeira, caviar and scented envelopes were things of the past.

The winter of 1917 was bitter and with coal supplies cut off Petrograd came to a frozen halt. The snow was piled, uncleared, on the city's streets for weeks on end. Gangs of robbers roamed the night streets, wearing white hoods with torchlights fixed by the eye-holes. They terrorized unwary passers-by, demanding not money but jewellery and warm clothing. The public health system collapsed completely and cholera broke out. Tiomkin was drafted into an anti-cholera squad responsible for disinfecting houses where the occupants had died of the disease. Spring brought some relief and the cholera epidemic was eventually brought under control. The Conservatoire even started to award its diplomas again. The war with Germany was over, but now there was a civil war to take its place.

Most members of the intelligentsia and the artistic community were liberal or liberal-socialist in their convictions and sympathies. However, many now joined with the Bolsheviks. It was a time of artistic as well as social upheaval and poets, playwrights and musicians collaborated on new forms of artistic presentation, reflecting the freshness and excitement of the Revolution. Yet, as Prokofiev and Shostakovich were to find, representing the Revolution in the arts was not an easy road to follow and Tiomkin's acquaintances from 'The Stray Dog': Meyerhold, now creating an international reputation for the Soviet theatre; Mayakovsky, abandoning futurism for propaganda; and Alexander Blok, hymning the Revolution in epic poetry – were soon to become disillusioned or fall from official favour. All three were to die young.

Like most of his circle, Tiomkin considered himself a liberal, and he regretted the passing of the democracy and personal freedom of the short-lived provisional government. Although he was aware that friends of his were involved in counter-Revolutionary movements, he knew that that way was not for him and he concentrated on his music and on simply staying alive.

He had been engaged to play the Skryabin Piano Concerto at a summer music festival near the Finnish border. While preparing his performance, he stayed with General Skirsky in Gachina on the outskirts of Petrograd. Tiomkin had made the acquaintance of the General, who was a gifted amateur musician, through the Conservatoire. One evening during Tiomkin's visit, some soldiers arrived and arrested Skirsky. As he was taken away, he said to Tiomkin, 'This is the end of me. I know it.'

Tiomkin managed to discover where Skirsky was being held and he was able to visit him in his cell which he was sharing with a number of former military leaders. However, when the time came for him to leave, the guard had been changed and, without an identification pass, Tiomkin himself could not be released. Three days passed and the evening of the concert performance came and went. Skirsky was taken from the prison, Tiomkin could only assume to be shot. (In fact the General perished when the steamship in which he was being transferred to another prison was blown up in transit).

It was not until Tiomkin heard one of his guards singing an old, familiar Ukranian song that he thought he might at long last have found a sympathetic ear for his plight. He played on the guard's nostalgic fondness for his home town of Poltava and its tiny river, the Psel. Eventually the Ukranian was persuaded to take a letter from Tiomkin to Glazunov explaining his predicament and begging for his help. His release was finally arranged, but when he went to thank Glazunov, he found the composer had left town on a journey.

The acute shortages of food and fuel continued. Foods that had been

In Berlin, early 1920s

scorned before the Revolution were now the height of luxury. Clothing too was scarce. Tiomkin had bartered so much of his wardrobe, including the splendid Conservatoire dress uniform, that he was now forced to make up a suit from a pair of heavy, brilliant green curtains.

After two years of deprivation, Tiomkin's health had begun to fail. He had lost a lot of weight and a persistent cough was threatening to develop into tuberculosis. His father had returned to Berlin after the Revolution and his mother now wrote to her former husband asking him to arrange an entry permit for their son. The Russian border was not yet sealed, but German visas were not easily come by. His father had influential friends in Germany and matters were quickly arranged through the German consulate in Petrograd. After a small farewell party, Tiomkin set off for Germany on a small freighter bound for Stettin. It was a rough crossing and the dozen or so passengers, all as undernourished and sickly as Tiomkin himself, suffered badly from sea-sickness. From Stettin, Tiomkin took the train to Berlin and finally arrived on his father's elegant doorstep, tired, dirty, emaciated, dressed in a suit made from green curtains and shoes made from off-cuts of rubber car-tyres.

The parting from his mother, with no hope of a reunion in the foreseeable future, had been a bitter blow. (Fortunately, she was eventually able to join her son in the United States, where she died in 1959.) She was a major influence on Tiomkin's life and music, and he was always conscious of the need to live up to her expectations of him. In later life he was fond of showing her framed photograph to his friends and even to comparative strangers. It bore the legend: 'God give me the serenity to accept the things I cannot change, the courage to change the things I can, and the wisdom to know the difference.' It was a precept he had always taken to heart and to the end of his life he never ceased to apply himself unstintingly and successfully to the acquisition of skills that did not necessarily come naturally to him.

Tiomkin and his father were now almost strangers to each other, and there was little willingness on the part of the father and his new young wife to welcome the exile into their home. Family relations were soon strained to breaking point. The father's adherence to the Germanic ideal, and his detestation of all things Russian, particularly Bolshevism, was anathema to the sensitive, musical youngster. Music was meaningless to Tiomkin's father and the sound of scales and arpeggios interrupting his medical consultations did not improve his temper. The crisis came when Tiomkin, feeling that his mother had been unfairly treated, launched a spirited defence of her. His father finally showed him the door.

Luckily, Tiomkin was not entirely alone and friendless in a strange country. He was never to forget the kindness shown him at this time by another relation, a cousin. She was also responsible for encouraging what were among Tiomkin's first efforts at composition when he set her topical verses to music as an enjoyable recreation for them both. He also now met up with an old friend from Petrograd, the pianist Kariton, who offered to share his apartment with him. Kariton had always been a shrewd gambler and he had a genius for wartime speculation. He had made a small fortune in Russia, and was now buying and selling goods at enormous profit, exploiting the chaotic economy of post-war Berlin.

He was lavishly generous and kept open house for Russian refugees, throwing extravagant parties where emigré artists mingled with the wealthy German middle class. He welcomed Tiomkin into his home and let him work at the piano all day long. Tiomkin entertained at the parties where Kariton lost no opportunity to pronounce on the bright future of the latest Russian genius of the keyboard. As he had been in St Petersburg, Tiomkin was soon full occupied teaching the piano to the daughters of rich Germans and emigré Russians. This brought him a reasonable income and he was soon able to move into an apartment of his own.

Through Kariton, Tiomkin met the German industrialist Deutsch who suggested a meeting with Busoni. It had long been an ambition of Tiomkin's to study with the legendary teacher and he could scarcely believe that all he had to do was to telephone for an appointment. He was given an interview and accepted as a pupil. Although Busoni could have easily made a fortune by taking any number of rich, and usually untalented, pupils, he compromised his artistic principles only so far as to accept the occasional large fee — often for doing little more than pondering a chess problem while ignoring the execrable playing of some millionaire's son — in order to subsidize his gifted pupils. Tiomkin did not have to pay a penny towards his tuition.

As Busoni was already old and in poor health, most of the instruction was given by his assistants, Egon Petri and Zadora. His system depended on a mechanical action in which the fingers were held almost flat. Tiomkin spent many painful months completely revising his technique. Busoni himself taught harmony, counterpoint and the philosophy of music. Tiomkin felt Busoni's approach to be the perfect complement of Glazunov's and a marvellous rounding off to his own musical education. Whereas Glazunov's influence had led towards a glowing romantic spirit, Busoni furnished Tiomkin with a strict, exact, musical discipline.

Tiomkin remained in Berlin for two and a half years, studying and teaching. A career as a concert pianist appeared to be opening up

Bureau de Concerts : MARCEL DE VALMALÈTE, 45, Rue La Boëtie, PARIS

Téléphone : Elysées 06-72 — Registre du Commerce Paris 209.955 B.

MAISON GAVEAU (Salle des Concerts), 45 - 47, RUE LA BOËTIE

DIMANCHE 15 JUIN 1924 à 21 heures

(Ouverture des portes à 20 h. 30)

CONCERT SYMPHONIQUE

ORCHESTRE de 70 MUSICIENS

sous la direction de

Vladimir GOLSCHMANN

Solistes :

Dimitri TIOMKINE
Michel KHARITON

PROGRAMME

I. Ouverture de Freischütz. . . . . WEBER

II. Concerto en la majeur (pour piano et orchestre) . . . . LISZT
   Adagio sostenuto assai. — Allegro agitato assai. — Allegro deciso
   Marciale un poco meno allegro — Allegro animato.
   (Ce concerto se joue sans interruption)
   Dimitri TIOMKINE et l'ORCHESTRE

ENTR'ACTE

III. 1er Concerto en si bémol mineur op. 23 (pour piano et orchestre) . . . . . TSCHAIKOWSKY
   Andante non troppo e molto maestoso. — Andantino simplice.
   Allegro con fuoco.
   Michel KHARITON et l'ORCHESTRE

IV. Capriccio Espagnol. . . . . RIMSKY-KORSAKOFF

V. 2e Suite pour deux pianos. . . . . RACHMANINOFF
   Introduction — Tempo di valse — Romance Tarentella.
   Dimitri TIOMKINE et Michel KHARITON

PIANOS GAVEAU

PRIX des PLACES : Parterre : Loges : 40 fr. ; Fauteuils : 40 et 30 fr. ; Premier Balcon, 15 et 10 fr. ;
Deuxième Balcon : 8 et 5 fr. ; Promenoirs, 3 fr. (droits compris).

BILLETS : MAISON GAVEAU 45-47, Rue La Boëtie. — chez DURAND, 4, Place de la Madeleine. — au GUIDE-BILLETS, 29,
Avenue de l'Opéra. — au BUREAU-MUSICAL, 52, Rue Tronchet. — chez ESCHIG, 48, rue de Rome. — SÉNART,
49, rue de Rome. ROUDANEZ, LAUDY, MAGASIN MUSICAL, etc...

Paris concert 1924

before him and he was engaged to play the Liszt A major Concerto with the Berlin Philharmonic. He also wrote and published light music — dances and marches — either anonymously or under a pseudonym. With Kariton, Tiomkin developed a two-piano partnership. At first they played together only at parties, but then Kariton in particular began to see the financial advantages of taking their act to Paris. Kariton engaged a Paris agent and negotiated a lucrative contract for a series of concerts. Until this point Tiomkin had never seriously considered money as important. Now, with Kariton's eloquent persuasion, he described himself as 'caught by the lure of money, some dormant instinct . . . was awakened'.

They chose their repertoire with an eye on the temperamental and technical balance between the two of them. Kariton's ebullience and fondness for danger, even violence – he was constantly provoking vicious knife-fights – was reflected in the iron wrists and steel fingers that gave tremendous power and resonance to his playing. Tiomkin's strength on the other hand was for lyrical, *cantabile* passages. Together they were a formidable team.

Paris was full of emigré Russians, many of them war profiteers flaunting their new money in the Left Bank cafés. But there were companies of Russian dancers, Russian musicians and Russian singers as well. The Russian arts were enjoying a considerable vogue in Paris in the wake of the Ballets Russes.

The Paris agent had made a good job of the advance publicity and their debut in one of the large concert halls was a sell-out. They were soon engaged for extra concerts and appearances at private parties. For the first time in his life Tiomkin knew what it was to feel rich. The agent had wisely advised them to expand their repertoire to include pieces by French composers. Tiomkin had become familiar with Debussy's music at 'The Stray Dog', and now began to study the work of Ravel, d'Indy, Dukas and Les Six, arranging a number of their pieces for two pianos.

There were many Americans in Paris at this time and Tiomkin renewed his acquaintance with the ragtime, blues and jazz he had got to know and love during his lessons with Miss Ruby in St Petersburg. Much as he wanted to play jazz himself, he found his academic, musical education inhibited his playing, the exactness of his rhythm sounding stiff and formal in comparison with the free, relaxed style of the American jazz bands he listened to so intently in the Paris cabarets.

The social gathering place in Paris for Russian artists was the salon of Madame Poliakov and it was there that Tiomkin met Chaliapin, whom he had known slightly in Russia. At this time Chaliapin was a great star at the Metropolitan Opera House in New York and he was able to open Tiomkin's eyes to a different side of American life from the world of speakeasies and Chicago gangsters that Tiomkin had absorbed through watching films and listening to Miss Ruby.

Chaliapin told Tiomkin that European musicians were in great demand in America for transcontinental tours. He himself was earning more at the Met. than even Caruso had done. Tiomkin was amazed and somewhat shocked to discover that on the vaudeville circuit serious musicians and dancers performed alongside comedians, acrobats and variety turns of all sorts. Chaliapin thought the two-piano act would work well in vaudeville, and he gave Tiomkin his first real lesson in showmanship, pointing out to him the time and place to make an effect and arouse the excitement and interest of an audience, independent of artistic considerations. Tiomkin began to think that this might be a skill worth acquiring.

The impresario Morris Gest, himself a Russian immigrant to the United States, heard Tiomkin and Kariton perform in Paris and offered them a three-month vaudeville tour in which they would be working with a ballet troupe. It was an unorthodox idea, but despite his initial misgivings Tiomkin accepted, estimating that he and Kariton could expect to return to Paris with ten thousand dollars' clear profit each at the end of the tour.

Albertina Rasch had been a prima ballerina in the opera in New York, Chicago and Boston. Now, partly in order to earn enough money to support her family back in Vienna, she had formed a ballet company of her own, the Albertina Rasch Dancers. It was this company that Tiomkin and Kariton were to work with. The billing read, 'Albertina Rasch presents... ' and as their producer it was Albertina who told the pianists what and how to play. She was the kind of crisp, business-like woman unknown in Europe at the time. She was cool and efficient with a natural precision and sense of authority; she was a woman of few words and spoke only when it was to the point. Kariton and Tiomkin took an instant dislike to her.

Tiomkin was outraged to find that Albertina was insisting on cuts being made in the music to accommodate the demands of vaudeville. To Tiomkin, brought up in the tradition of Glazunov and Busoni, excising twelve bars of Chopin here or twenty bars of Rachmaninov there was a sacrilege. The other demand Albertina made of him was the simplest of orchestrations for the resident theatre orchestra of the last dozen or so bars of the concluding number to produce a rousing and effective finale. She addressed herself exclusively to Tiomkin, judging him the more musical of the pair and recognizing in him an ability to appreciate the relationship between music and gesture, an understanding he had developed during the tour with Karsavina in the early months of the Revolution. Kariton on the other hand was

completely ignored by Albertina and his one thought was how they were going to get rid of her.

While in New York, Tiomkin again met Prince Obolensky, now divorced from the Princess and married to Alice Astor. Obolensky decided to turn the debut of the Albertina Rasch Dancers and the two Russian pianists into a high spot in the New York social calendar. Albertina and Morris Gest capitalized on the connection with Obolensky and scheduled the two-piano act as the finale of the programme. Kariton's complete command of audience-rousing showmanship ensured a wild ovation from the high society audience.

Throughout his vaudeville career, Tiomkin found it almost impossible to come to terms with the showmanship that was demanded of him. All his training, from his classes with Professor Blumenfeld at the St Petersburg Conservatoire onwards, had been geared towards a discreet, reserved style of presentation that allowed the music to speak for itself. Blumenfeld had insisted on the minimum of movement when playing and Busoni had been bitingly scornful of any suggestion of exhibitionism.

The flamboyant, tricksy style that vaudeville required came naturally to Kariton and his platform behaviour — flinging his hand out at the top of a run, raising his hands high before a loud chord, sinking hunched over the keyboard in exquisite agony, tossing his head and shoulders backwards in passion or ecstasy, while still managing to smile occasionally at the audience or to make eyes at a girl in the front row — was exactly what was needed. Tiomkin did what he could to keep pace with the histrionics, which even included edging the piano itself nearer and nearer to the front of the stage, but finally he had to concede defeat. Albertina understood Tiomkin's distaste but encouraged him to keep working on his stage presentation, comforting him with the thought that the thousand dollar pay cheque at the end of each week was compensation enough for the assault on his artistic sensibilities.

Albertina also encouraged Tiomkin's attempts to master the English language. Although he had learned French and German at school, English was new to him. Not only the pronunciation, but the syntax and word order provided almost insurmountable obstacles for him. In fact, once Tiomkin had absorbed a large enough vocabulary to make himself understood, his concern for correct grammar vanished

◁ *With Albertina, late 1920s*

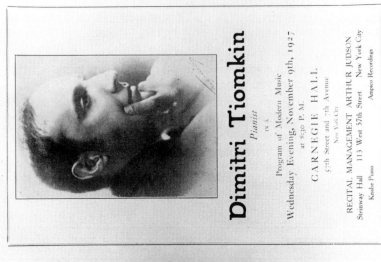

PROGRAM

I.

I. Sonata No. 4, for Piano .... *J. Scriabin*

II.

II. Suite for Piano .... *Francis Poulenc*
(First time in America)

   (a) Presto
   (b) Andante
   (c) Vif.
   (Played without a pause)

III. Mouvements Perpetuals for Piano .... *Francis Poulenc*

   (a) Balance Modere
   (b) Modere
   (c) Alerte

VI. Sonatine for Piano .... *Alexandre Tansman*
(First time in America)

   (a) Modere
   (b) In Modo Polonico
   (c) Toccata

III.

V. Melodie .... *Alexandre Tansman*

VI. Humoresque

VII. Mazurka No. 4 .... *Alexandre Tansman*
(First time anywhere)

VIII. The Flight of the Bumble-Bee .... *Rimsky-Korsakoff*
(Concert arrangement for Piano by Joseph Strimer)
(First time in America)

III.

IX. Quasi-Jazz .... *Dimitri Tiomkin*

X. Secret .... *F. Mompou*
(First time in America)

XI. Gitana

XII. (a) Toccata
   (b) Oiseau Tristes
   (c) Minuet .... *Ravel*
   (dedicated to Haydn)
   (d) La Valse
   (Poeme Choregraphique)
   (Transcription for Piano by the Composer)
   (First performance on the Piano in America)

Application Form for Tickets

Please send .... tickets for the Recital of Dimitri Tiomkin for
which I enclose cheque for .... dollars.

Prices: $2.20, $1.65, $1.10, 75c: including tax

Name ....

Address ....

Note, all cheques payable to Recital Management Arthur Judson, Steinway Hall, 113 W. 57th Street, New York City

Dimitri Tiomkin

Pianist

IN A

Program of Modern Music

Wednesday Evening, November 9th, 1927

at 8:30 P. M.

CARNEGIE HALL

57th Street and 7th Avenue
New York City

RECITAL MANAGEMENT ARTHUR JUDSON

Steinway Hall   113 West 57th Street   New York City

Knabe Piano   Ampico Recordings

Carnegie Hall recital 1927

completely and for the rest of his life his vivid and colourful style of expression was to give much delight and amusement.

Albertina set to work Americanizing Tiomkin, and one thing that had to go was his excessive, florid courtesy. Out went his habit of kissing a woman's hand on introduction and out went the slightly mincing walk that was the epitome of elegance in old Russia. In came a controlled casualness, the hat on the back of the head, a manly stride and a firm hand-shake.

By the end of the tour, relations had become slightly strained between the two pianists and their desire to move in different musical directions had become more apparent. The tour had been a financial success, but now Tiomkin wanted to return to the recital platform. Moreover, he was planning to stay in America, take out citizenship papers — although he did not actually become an American citizen until 1937 — and marry Albertina Rasch. It was the end of the two-piano act.

Tiomkin was now in the homeland of jazz and the more he heard of it, the more it fascinated him and the more he wanted to be able to play it himself. Albertina had a piano-roll recording of Gershwin's *Rhapsody in Blue* and Tiomkin played it over and over again. His attempts to teach himself jazz piano had all been doomed to failure and when he heard the black pianist Henderson on the radio he wrote to him asking for lessons. Henderson had had no formal musical training himself and Tiomkin struggled to unlearn the discipline of strict tempo and to absorb the syncopations and irregular pulses of modern jazz. He looked on his studies with Henderson as a postgraduate course, a performer's finishing school.

Tiomkin's interest in jazz began to influence Albertina in her choice of music for her troupe of dancers. Tiomkin was now confident of his new piano style and the two planned a ballet to *Rhapsody in Blue* with Tiomkin at the piano. Gershwin himself dropped in on the rehearsals but, much to Tiomkin's disappointment, he seemed more interested in being photographed with the dancers than in hearing Tiomkin's interpretation of his music.

Tiomkin began to work seriously on the concert repertoire, attracting attention with programmes of new music and American premieres rather than the standard repertoire. He introduced music by composers such as Poulenc and Ravel (a piano transcription of *La Valse*, for example) to New York audiences and also included some short pieces of his own, *Quasi-jazz* and *Impression of the Blues* among them, in his programmes. After a recital at the Carnegie Hall, Tiomkin decided to take advantage of Albertina's visit to Paris — some of her dancers were booked at the Moulin Rouge — to accompany her and to investigate the possibilities for building a European reputation as a concert pianist which could only further his American career.

While in France he gave a number of recitals, but the music that was so new to New York was comfortably familiar to Paris concert-goers. The solution appeared to be to plan American programmes for Europe and it was not until his return to New York that the idea occurred to him to offer an all-Gershwin concert, with not only the *Rhapsody in Blue*, but also the F major Concerto, which had not yet been made available for performance by Gershwin's publishers. Tiomkin made an appointment to meet Gershwin and the composer welcomed him to his grand house with old-world charm and courtesy. He was delighted by the suggestion of a Paris concert and promised Tiomkin the set of manuscript orchestral parts.

Once the business had been concluded, Gershwin moved to his piano and played some of his own compositions. It was a performance Tiomkin remembered vividly: 'His pianism was of a piece with his compositions. — little schooled but inspired. Though lacking in method and technique, his hands seemed to blend with the keyboard, as if his fingers had an organic unity with the keys and the music flowed from them. His whole body moved with his hands and the music, swaying, bending, twisting. There was no suggestion of exhibitionism or showmanship. Rather, you were reminded of some blithesome person who seems to dance as he walks. It was musical magic, Gershwin playing Gershwin.'

Success had come easily to George Gershwin. In his mid-thirties, he could look back on a long series of triumphs. His success resulted in a supreme self-confidence that seemed at times almost arrogant. He was gracious and charming in company and much sought after by New York society.

Albertina and Tiomkin began to plan the most effective way of mounting the Paris concert. Through friends they were able to book the Paris Opéra, the shrine of French serious music, enough of a publicity coup in itself. Gershwin was expected to attend the concert in person and Albertina and Tiomkin travelled to Paris in March 1928, six weeks prior to the event, to organize the concert promotion personally. They leased a fashionable apartment in the Champs Elysées, hired a professional French cook and set about entertaining the Parisian musicians and critics. Tiomkin's Paris agent had already begun a carefully organized publicity drive, exciting curiosity about the

L'Administration de Concerts **A.** **D**andelot et **F**ils annonce la venue des **C**élèbres **A**rtistes

TITTA RUFFO

au Théâtre des Champs-Élysées

Lundi 7 Mai

W. FURTWÄNGLER

et l'Orchestre Philharmonique
de Berlin

à la Salle Pleyel, le 11 Mai

BRAILOWSKY

(Récital Chopin)

Opéra, Mardi 22 Mai

GODOWSKY

à

l'Opéra, le Jeudi 24 Mai

J. HEIFETZ

Salle Pleyel 6 Juin

Opéra 19 Juin

D. TIOMKIN

Opéra, Mardi 29 Mai soirée

et Samedi 9 Juin en matinée

Programmes détaillés et location chez MM. A. DANDELOT et Fils, *85, rue d'Amsterdam* - (Gut. 15-25)

Paris handbill, 1928

forthcoming musical sensation.

Albertina was no mean cook herself, and in conjunction with a Madame Forrestier an irresistible buffet menu was devised for the party that was planned as the culmination of weeks of advance publicity. The Tiomkins were now growing anxious about the advisability of an all-Gershwin concert and decided finally on two concerts, a week apart, with one Gershwin concerto in each, balanced by a concerto from the standard repertoire.

Gershwin arrived in Paris in time for the first rehearsals and became a frequent visitor to the Tiomkin's apartment. The conductor, Vladimir Golschmann, coaxed the dignified French musicians through the unfamiliar jazz rhythms, but revolt finally erupted when the trumpet-players were called upon to use derby hats as mutes to produce the characteristic wah-wah sound. They were pacified only when the hats were shorn of their rims and painted gold.

The bold concert planning of combining Liszt's A major Concerto with Gershwin's Concerto in F and the razzmatazz of advance publicity brought their rewards. The audience was full of such figures as Diaghilev, Prokofiev, Arthur Honegger and Maurice Chevalier. The concert was widely reported in the press and Tiomkin became an instant celebrity. The second of the two concerts placed the *Rhapsody in Blue* alongside a Mozart Concerto and firmly established Gershwin in European musical circles.

During their stay in Paris, the Tiomkins saw a lot of Ravel, remembered by Tiomkin as 'birdlike', 'absent-minded' and 'naïve'. Ravel was much impressed by Gershwin's music and the two became firm friends. Gershwin, very conscious of his lack of formal musical education, was anxious to study with Ravel, but Ravel declined to teach him with the question, 'Why make a bad Ravel out of a good Gershwin?'

The original aim of the Paris venture, to create a stir in Europe that would result in engagements back in the States, was wholly successful. On his return to America, Tiomkin played the *Rhapsody in Blue* at the Carnegie Hall and reverted to his specialist repertoire of contemporary French composers for a cross-country recital tour at the kind of fee unthinkable before his Parisian triumph. In time Tiomkin was to see his interest in jazz as a temporary phase in his development as a pianist and composer. Writing and performing jazz were new skills that he had acquired, but he no longer viewed them as ends in themselves.

Tiomkin and Albertina settled into a busy and successful routine, with Albertina directing her ballet school and staging Broadway shows,

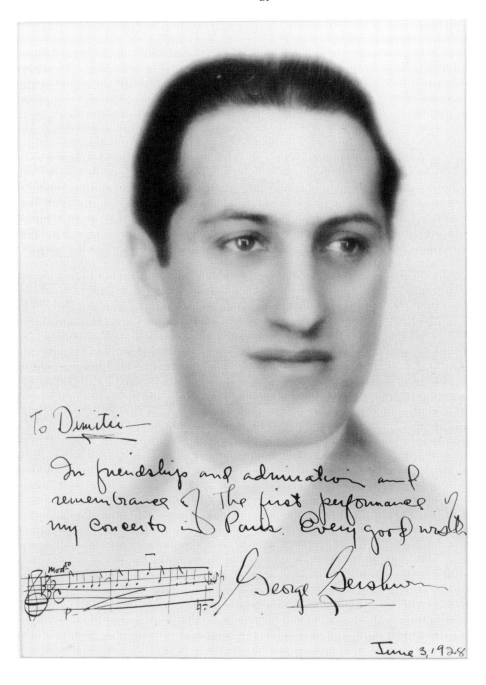

Gershwin dedication, 1928

Arthur Lange conducting one of Tiomkin's early MGM compositions

while Tiomkin travelled the country giving piano recitals. However, the Depression of 1929 soon changed their way of life. Money was scarce in all quarters and engagements for dancers and pianists were few and far between.

Albertina had already worked once or twice in Hollywood and she was now invited to produce a series of ballets for films. Tiomkin moved with her to California. Although he continued to give occasional recitals, still championing the music of Busoni, Ravel, Mompou, Tansman and Gershwin, Tiomkin's interest in composition now began to develop. He was writing at this period in no particular style and for various media, and his compositions ranged from light songs to serious orchestral works. He played some of his own music in his recitals and he also occasionally wrote numbers for the Albertina Rasch Dancers, but he was depressed to find that he was unable to interest any music publishers in his work.

One piece he had written for the Dancers was the *Mars Ballet*. Albertina mentioned the work to her colleagues at the film studio, but

Tiomkin flatly refused to play the piece for them, insisting that it was not the composer's business to plug his wares like a door-to-door salesman. Arthur Zepp had worked as a butler for the Tiomkins almost since their marriage. He had been a lift-boy with musical aspirations and Tiomkin had taken pity on him and offered him a job with access to a piano as an additional perk. Zepp volunteered to play the *Mars Ballet* to the studio heads.

The *Mars Ballet* was sold to the studio for three thousand dollars and Tiomkin was commissioned to write several more pieces. Almost by accident he had become a composer of film music. Hollywood was the one place in America where musicians, both composers and performers, were largely untouched by the Depression. Live theatre music to accompany films was being phased out and replaced by a recorded soundtrack. There was plenty of work for everyone.

Tiomkin describes his first assignment for a screenplay as 'the last word in the obvious'. Universal was making a sound-film version of Tolstoy's *Resurrection* and who better than a Russian to write music with an authentic Russian flavour? While none too happy about his own work — 'a concoction of some Russian tunes in minor keys and a lot of standard sentimentality in the style of Romberg's musical comedies' — this first film taught Tiomkin the bitter lesson of what can happen to a score in the hands of engineers. Music he had imagined as quiet and expressive was drowned out by the sound effects and his expansive, *fortissimo* passages were faded almost to a whisper.

At this time Tiomkin was finding his other musical career — as a concert pianist — less and less satisfying. He was beginning to become depressed by the demands of small-town society. When he was out on tour, his engagement did not end with the conclusion of his recital; he was then required to attend parties and receptions which he found boring. Back in New York, he once more struck out in a new direction, making a brief sortie into the world of theatrical management. He went into partnership with Montague Glass, the creator of the strip-cartoon characters, the Jewish businessmen Potash and Perlmutter. In the absence of other backers, Tiomkin and Glass resolved to produce Glass's play, *Cutting Expenses Down*, themselves. They booked a theatre owned by Lee Shubert and set up office in Albertina's studio. *Cutting Expenses Down* ran only for five days, during which short time Tiomkin turned down an offer for the motion picture rights.

Tiomkin moved the stage-set of office furniture into a rented office and set himself up as a Broadway producer. His next project was a musical called *Aha!* for which he wrote the music and Newman Levy the lyrics. Morris Gest was interested in producing it, but he died before the piece could be staged. Another project halted by Gest's death was the hiring of the Winter Garden for a repertory season of musicals, plays and opera. The Depression was no time for grand theatrical ideas and Tiomkin's career as a Broadway producer was short-lived. During this slack period, however, the energetic Tiomkin was far from idle. Many of the songs and themes he wrote during this time, either for his own amusement or for projected musicals, such as the one he wrote with Henry Meyers on Nell Gwynn, were to resurface later, sometimes with scarcely a note altered, in his film scores. In the meantime Albertina had been occupying herself with a non-artistic venture, namely the opening of what was called the Albertina Rasch Tea Room, situated a few blocks away from Carnegie Hall. According to her husband its success was short-lived as a result of Albertina's fondness for giving away boxes of expensive chocolates as presents to her many distinguished patrons; nevertheless the 'Russian Tea Room' stands on its site and flourishes to this day.

The film industry had been among the last to succumb to the stringencies of the Depression and now it was among the first to recover. In 1933 Tiomkin was summoned back to Hollywood to work on the Paramount picture *Alice in Wonderland*. Whereas Tiomkin had been the obvious choice of composer for *Resurrection*, commissioning him to write the score for *Alice* had a certain Carrollian inconsequence of its own. Tiomkin was comfortable with the kind of quaint English musical idiom required, and was able to make use of his studies in earlier music, most notably of Purcell and madrigal-writing, in his score for the film. However, his appreciation of the intricacies of spoken English and in particular of Lewis Carroll's personal brand of high nonsense was quite another matter. Characteristically determined to set Carroll's words as faithfully as possible, Tiomkin spent many concentrated hours notating the precise time-values and stresses as he persuaded friends and acquaintances to recite over and over such lines as 'Beware the Jabberwock, my son' or 'How doth the little crocodile improve his shining tail?'

Alice in Wonderland was followed by a number of scores for pictures which, while not engaging Tiomkin's talents to the full, brought him a comfortable income. Tiomkin and Albertina now joined the Hollywood social round and it was at a party given by the writer Joe Swerling that they met Frank Capra. There was an immediate warmth between the two men. Capra was fond of music, particularly Italian opera, and Tiomkin had found a kindred spirit, a man who shared his own sense of the ridiculous and yet who was also inclined to a degree of sentimentality. Capra's wife, Lucille, and Albertina also became great friends and soon the four were almost inseparable.

Their friendship survived the fact that Capra had not particularly liked Tiomkin's score for *Alice in Wonderland* and it was not until 1937 and *Lost Horizon* that Capra invited Tiomkin to work with him. It was the perfect opportunity for Tiomkin. He was given an almost free hand and allowed a large chorus and orchestra. The one disagreement between Tiomkin and Capra over the music for the film came with the scoring for the death of the Lama. Capra's instinct was to reflect the purity of the character with the simplest of musical means. But Tiomkin wanted to reinforce the sense of immense loss and shared grief with a *marcia funebre* calling for enormous choral and orchestral forces. Capra was eventually converted to the idea, although it was not until some years later that he actually admitted to Tiomkin that he, Tiomkin, had been right.

It was to Capra that Tiomkin owed his discovery of indigenous

Recording Lost Horizon *(l. to r.) Capra, Columbia Musical Director Morris Stoloff, Max Steiner, Tiomkin*

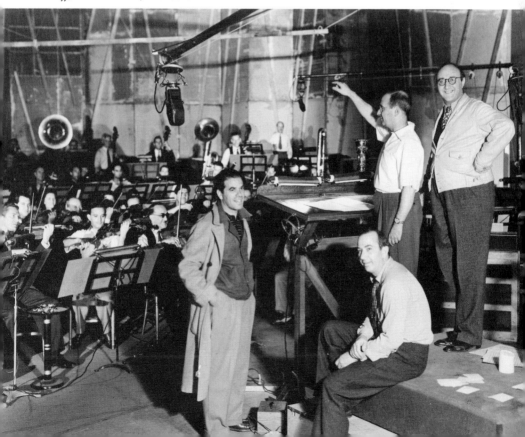

American music. Capra was himself an immigrant and he had become fascinated by the history and folklore of his adopted homeland. At this time the idea of American music meant only jazz as far as Tiomkin was concerned, but now Capra introduced him to Appalachian folksong, New England hymns and the working songs sung by cowboys and railroad pioneers. One collection of songs that Capra showed to Tiomkin, called *What America Sings*, included not only selections from Mendelssohn and Gounod, but also New England fiddler tunes, Negro spirituals and eighteenth-century ballads. With his appetite for American music thoroughly whetted, Tiomkin was able to pursue his own studies, becoming familiar with the songs of lumberjacks and cotton plantation slaves as well as sea shanties and barn dances. Soon he could accurately reproduce the essential spirit of these different popular musical styles, and whenever a film called for a negro spiritual or hillbilly song, Tiomkin was ready to provide exactly what was wanted.

Lost Horizon was a great success for all concerned in its making, and Tiomkin was offered films by several producers, including Sam Goldwyn. He had as much work as he cared to accept. One of his next films was *The Great Waltz* for which he was required to edit, re-work and run together the best known works of Johann Strauss, who was perpetually confused in the minds of some of the studio heads with Oscar Straus and even Richard Strauss. The essence of the film was, as Tiomkin himself put it, 'eternal youth in three-quarter time'.

A further opportunity came to expand his knowledge of truly American music with Henry Hathaway's *Spawn of the North*, a film set among Alaskan Indian salmon fishermen. Hathaway used almost a documentary approach in his fiction films and Tiomkin welcomed the opportunity to work towards a parallel musical authenticity. His solution was an extended jam session with Californian and Mexican Indians improvising round a tune Tiomkin had written in the correct pentatonic mode. The session was lubricated with quantities of the best Russian vodka. The resultant score, while far from truly Alaskan, gave the required impression of authenticity.

In fact this apparent authenticity was something that caught the ear of Prokofiev when he paid a visit to Paramount Studios in 1938. This was his last journey abroad, and he acquired in Hollywood some valuable knowledge in the sphere of sound-recording techniques which, back in Moscow, he put to good use in realising his score for Eisentein's *Alexander Nevsky* (parts of which, incidentally, Tiomkin was to incorporate in his 1945 *Battle of Russia*). Prokofiev and Tiomkin were introduced on the music-scoring stage and spoke in Russian, but although they had not seen each other for some twenty years their meeting was strangely formal and neither of them mentioned the days of their youth in St Petersburg, the 'Stray Dog' and the Conservatoire. Tiomkin recognized Prokofiev's restraint as a kind of caution. Although Stalin's purges had not yet reached their height and artists were still relatively free, contact with the West, and particularly with Russian emigrés such as Tiomkin, was hardly advisable for an 'approved' Soviet composer. However, Prokofiev was able to express his enthusiasm for Tiomkin's 'truly aboriginal' score and his delight in discovering the extraordinary sonority of the Indian double flute.

The publicity surrounding *Lost Horizon* reminded promoters of Tiomkin the concert pianist and he was willingly lured back to the concert platform, hoping to balance his two careers of performer and composer. Soon he was playing his favourite Rachmaninov Concerto with the Los Angeles Symphony conducted by Albert Coates. Sadly, a broken arm finally put an end to his performing career. He fell on a friend's lawn and, although the injury did not at first appear serious, when the bone had healed the movement in his hand was slightly restricted. Virtuoso performance was no longer possible.

The pull of the concert platform was still strong, and Tiomkin began to admit to an ambition he had long been nursing to himself: he wanted to conduct. He was depressed by the lack of musical sensitivity in the orchestral conductors he had to work with at the film studios. Their main concern appeared to be precise timing and they tended to disregard the dynamics of the score, not appreciating that the music had been crafted deliberately in order to heighten or point a desired dramatic effect.

Already Tiomkin was developing a reputation for being 'difficult' at recording sessions, insisting on orchestral balance, phrasing and expression, and he now began to feel that he might as well be conducting his own music himself. As ever, when it was a matter of acquiring a new skill, Tiomkin turned to the nearest available expert, on this occasion Mischa Bakaleinikoff, a double-bass player who was used to conducting light opera back in his native Russia. From Bakaleinikoff Tiomkin learned the basic techniques of synchronizing music and film with the baton.

He made his conducting debut in the Hollywood Bowl, sharing the programme with the Albertina Rasch Dancers. He conducted excerpts from his own score for *Lost Horizon*, but Albertina was not yet

Tuesday Concert, Aug. 16, 8:30 P. M.

SOUTHERN CALIFORNIA SYMPHONY ASSOCIATION

Presents

ALBERTINA RASCH BALLET

LOS ANGELES PHILHARMONIC ORCHESTRA

★

DIMITRI TIOMKIN and ARTHUR GUTTMANN
Conductors

and the

HALL JOHNSON CHOIR
(All choral arrangements by Hall Johnson)

★

Overture, Merry Wives of Windsor	Nicolai
Excerpts from "The Great Waltz"	Strauss-Tiomkin
(Courtesy of Metro-Goldwyn-Mayer)	
ALBERTINA RASCH BALLET	

(Intermission 15 Minutes)

Suite of "The Lost Horizon"   Tiomkin
(Courtesy of Columbia Pictures)
Conducted by the Composer
Assisted by the HALL JOHNSON CHOIR
Prelude
Mongolian Camp
Mountain Passage
Arrival in Shangri La
Doves of Sandra
Riding Through the Valley of the Blue Moon
Children's Pranks
Meditation
High Lama's Death
Funeral Procession
Lost in the Snow
Epilogue

Roumanian Rhapsody   Enesco
ALBERTINA RASCH BALLET

Page Thirteen

Tiomkin's conducting debut at the Hollywood Bowl, 16 August 1938 (from the Hollywood Bowl Magazine) prepared to entrust the music for her dancers to her husband's novice conducting.

Tiomkin then began to conduct some of his film music at recording sessions. At first he conducted only in the minor studios, sometimes taking on work for second-rate films at small fees simply in order to gain conducting experience. In his own eyes he never became a good conductor and his beat was not always clear. Conducting for him was always hard work, and rarely enjoyable. He regretted his lack of a spectacular style and that he did not cut an electrifying figure on the podium; his stance he described as 'a little hunched over' and his beat as 'musclebound'. He achieved his results through refusing to be hurried or otherwise pressurized; large numbers of sessions were always *de rigueur*, and no expense was spared in doing justice to whatever he felt the requirements of a film to be. A first-hand account of Tiomkin at work is provided by the British percussionist, James Blades, in his autobiography, *Drum Roll*:

> To those who know him, Dimitri is a lovable character and a most friendly man. He fears no one, however, and I must say that he can at times be particularly exasperating. On more than one occasion he has made me play a single note on a timpano at least twenty times, but finally noticing an unusual glint in my eye he would approve and say, 'Jimmy, I love you.' I was not alone in having to play a single note time and time again. Whilst working on the music for *The Guns of Navarone*, Dimitri questioned the sound of a chord on the piano. Now, the pianist Robert Docker is a pianist who can play a thousand chords in succession and every one a 'pearl'. This Dimitri knew well, so he said, 'It is the piano — get in another one.' When the producer said that to get another one would cost nearly £500 Dimitri barked, '£500, what is £500? — this film will make a million.' How right he was, and how right this grand musician was when, excusing a group of six percussionists their difficulty in getting their strokes absolutely together, he said, 'One sometimes makes the mistake of putting too many plonking instruments together.'

Most of Tiomkin's conducting was of course done in a sound studio, rather than in a concert hall in front of an audience, with all the peculiarly demanding considerations of recording music for film. Tiomkin described the challenging and anxiety-ridden activity as follows:

> Some great maestro might tell you that motion picture conducting is easy. Let him try it. Suppose you are scoring the picture, which

runs on a screen behind the orchestra. You watch the action on the film as you beat time, making sure that the music matches the scenes. In an opera the singers and the action follow the beat of the conductor; but film runs at a constant speed, and you have to follow that. The dialogue and action won't wait for you. You're on an inexorable treadmill; yet you must make the music sound expressive and spontaneous. Too rigid a tempo will sound mechanical; but if you take liberties, the picture may run away from you.

It was for another film for Frank Capra, *Meet John Doe*, that Tiomkin at last conducted his own score for a major studio. Capra was sensitive to the increasing threat of Fascism within the United States itself, and in *Meet John Doe* he explored the danger through the situation of an idealist, dedicated to the concept of individual freedom, who is faced with the forces of oppression embodied in a corporation president. The climax of the film had the hero sacrificing himself by jumping to his death in order to save mankind. This heavily symbolic conclusion was supported by Tiomkin's paraphrase of the Negro spiritual 'Deep River' and the 'Ode to Joy' from Beethoven's Ninth Symphony. It was a scene of extraordinary intensity and emotion.

Tiomkin was shattered to discover, after the first private showing of the film, that the entire ending was to be axed and an alternative scene, in which the corporation president suddenly and inexplicably sees the light and restrains the hero from committing suicide, was to be substituted. To Tiomkin this was a ludicrous and false conclusion, whereas the original had been noble, tragic and honest. Capra's point was that the pessimism of the original was unsuitable for wartime audiences. Tiomkin found himself unable to accept the compromise and felt disillusioned with Capra, whose integrity he had hitherto greatly respected.

When America entered the war Tiomkin was passed as unfit for military service and so he was particularly delighted to be invited by Capra to join the Army Film Center in Hollywood. For Tiomkin it was a kind of paradise, one of the busiest and most satisfying periods of his working life. The Unit made hundreds of films, ranging from short training films to full-blown propaganda epics. Tiomkin could call on whatever instrumental forces he liked and, freed from the pressure of studio budgets, crews now worked round the clock. At the Army Film Center, the film-makers were working against time and in order to achieve a specific audience response. Tiomkin acquired new skills along with a vast amount of experience.

Tiomkin happily committed himself to the propaganda element of his work, particularly in a series of films made to bring conditions inside the countries who were America's allies during the Second World War into the consiousness of Americans whose own lives seemed for a long time to be almost untouched by the European confrontation. Most potent of all in this series, for Tiomkin, was *The Battle of Russia*. Time and again he was reduced to tears as he sat watching thousands of feet of Soviet war film of the Nazi invasion and the Russian resistance:

> I sat for hours watching the scenes of war and devastation in Russia, my native land. One lot of film showed the desperate fighting in the Ukraine.... I saw destruction and horror in Kiev, the old capital, the sweep of war across the steppes. . . . Most affecting of all was the siege of Leningrad – scenes of havoc, the city under bombardment. . . . There was the Italianate architecture, some of it shattered, the broad avenues littered with wreckage, the River Neva still flowing placidly. I recognized this neighbourhood and that, one building after another. I had memories of the Conservatoire, students in uniforms with dress swords, Glazunov. There on the screen was the neighbourhood of 'The Stray Dog' . . . where we talked endlessly of art and danced to 'Alexander's Ragtime Band'.

To do justice to this powerful newsreel footage, Tiomkin assembled a score from the greatest works of Mussorgsky, Borodin, Tchaikovsky, Rimsky-Korsakov, Prokofiev and Glazunov. The customary army musicians were augmented by an Air Force orchestra and a large chorus. In order to accommodate all these musicians, the recordings had to be moved to the Paramount Studios.

The end of the war found Hollywood booming and Tiomkin full of energy and ambition. The next twenty years were to see a remarkable series of persuasive and impressive film scores. It was a period during which Tiomkin worked with the greatest names in Hollywood, including Wyler (*Friendly Persuasion*), Hitchcock (*Shadow of a Doubt, Dial M for Murder, I Confess*), Howard Hawks (*Red River, The Big Sky, The Thing, Land of the Pharaohs, Rio Bravo*), Carl Foreman (*High Noon, Cyrano de Bergerac, Champion, The Men, The Guns of Navarone*) and Samuel Bronston (*55 Days at Peking, The Fall of the Roman Empire* and *Circus World*). But Frank Capra was not of their number. After the war he had returned to making straightforward entertainment films, forming his own independent production company, Liberty Pictures, in order to do so. The last film on which he and Tiomkin worked

High Noon - *Tex Ritter*

(l. to r.) Alfred Newman, lyricist Ned Washington and Tiomkin who has just been presented with his two Oscars for High Noon *by Walt Disney (far right)*

together was *It's a Wonderful Life*. Tiomkin was greatly depressed to find that, after his music had been dubbed on to the soundtrack, Capra had then re-edited it, switching sections around and inserting music by other composers. Tiomkin had previously enjoyed working with Capra and being left, as he thought, to exercise his own discretion when it came to the music. He now felt betrayed by Capra and no longer had any interest in the film, or indeed in working with him again.

The complaint that directors interfere in the work of their fellow creative artists is a familiar one in the film world and now, in Tiomkin's eyes, Capra had joined the ranks of the 'big-time directors [who] make themselves writers, musicians, everything; they revamp dialogue, and cut and shuffle the music track to suit their fancy. It would not matter if it were only a case of tunes; but it is unendurable when the music is composed and has structure.'

Tiomkin was no innocent in regard to Hollywood economics, and in the post-war boom he deliberately set out to make money from his music. He proved to be an acute businessman and a skilled negotiator.

'An apotheosis', claimed Tiomkin 'when a composer gets his name on the marquee!'

He was the first composer to negotiate a flat fee with additional payments for extra music over and above a pre-arranged duration. His fee of $50,000 for *The Guns of Navarone* in 1961 was a record for the film industry at the time, and he was also a vociferous proponent of composers receiving percentages of gramophone-record and music-publishing royalties.

High Noon (1952) brought him his first two Oscars. *High Noon* had been produced by Stanley Kramer and Carl Foreman before they had left the Hollywood Motion Picture Center. The film was designed as a western but the balance between realism and romance was proving uncomfortable for the distributors. Gary Cooper did not appear to belong in the mould of a classical western hero and the studio heads hoped that the unifying element of a strong musical score might help to engage an audience. Tiomkin thought the key to the problem might be a song that could be sung, whistled or orchestrated, reappearing in different guises throughout the film. The result was 'Do not forsake me' and it won Tiomkin an Oscar not only for the best motion picture score, but for the best motion picture song. A third Oscar followed three years later, this time for the score of *The High and the Mighty*, a fourth in 1958 for *The Old Man and the Sea*.

These awards meant a great deal to Tiomkin and he never sought to appear blasé about the honours and recognition accorded him by his fellow film professionals. He devoted an entire room in the Highgate house where he spent his last years to his collection of mementoes of his life in films, including his Oscars and scores of signed photographs given to him by stars and directors. Among his most treasured possessions was a small Mexican violin, a gift from John Wayne.

At the Academy Award ceremony in 1955, when he won an Oscar for *The High and the Mighty*, Tiomkin unwittingly succeeded in sending up the recognized convention whereby the recipient gratefully acknowledged the part played in his own achievement by everyone working on the film, from the director to the tea-boy. His intention however had been somewhat different. The theme of *The High and the Mighty* had recently been the subject of a court case in which Tiomkin had been accused of plagiarism. Tiomkin had won the case, chiefly by virtue of the testimony of Dr Sigmund Spaeth, the self-styled 'Tune Detective'. It was Spaeth's contention that there was nothing new under the sun when it came to the component units of a melodic line. He was renowned for his exposition of the origins of 'Yes, we have no bananas' as a combination of 'My bonnie lies over the ocean', *The Bohemian Girl*, and Handel's *Messiah*. Spaeth applied the same treatment to Tiomkin's theme, revealing its roots in the works of the great classical composers of the previous two hundred years.

Thus Tiomkin was able, with utter seriousness, to list the names of the people to whom he wished to attribute his success, not only in the film studio but also, by implication, in the court-room. 'I like to thank Johannes Brahms, Johann Strauss, Richard Strauss, Richard Wagner, Beethoven, Rimsky-Korsakov . . . ' The remainder of the list was drowned by delighted applause, laughter, cheers and Bob Hope's 'You'll never get on *this* show again. . . . ' (Hope was to be proved wrong when Tiomkin collected his fourth Oscar for *The Old Man and the Sea*).

Following the success of 'Do not forsake me', sung by Tex Ritter, Tiomkin turned consciously to writing songs aimed at the hit parade. The tender 'Thee I Love' from the Quaker film, *Friendly Persuasion*, was a case in point. All concerned were hoping for a repetition of the runaway success of 'Do not forsake me'. First choice for the singer was Perry Como, already a well-established television and recording star.

Friendly Persuasion — *William Wyler, Gary Cooper, Tiomkin, Jester Hairston*
(holding music)

The studio had allowed a budget of $2,500, but when Tiomkin rang Como's agent to negotiate a fee, he found himself offering the singer $15,000 as a starting figure for discussion. The agent apparently agreed the fee and Tiomkin spent the night in some trepidation, anticipating the reaction at the studio the next day when it was discovered how cavalier he had been with the budget. However, when Como's agent rang to confirm the fee, it transpired that he had misheard Tiomkin and understood Como was being offered $50,000. Eventually the then unknown Pat Boone was discovered on a television talent show and engaged for only $3,000. His relaxed and unsophisticated style proved perfect for the song; his recording sold nearly one and a half million copies, and launched him on his highly successful career.

The subject of Otto Preminger's *The Court-Martial of Billy Mitchell* caught the imagination of Tiomkin and his lyric writer on the film, Paul Francis Webster. Billy Mitchell was the far-sighted army general who could clearly see the future importance of air power to modern warfare and that the battle for the skies would be the key to dominance on land and sea. Cassandra-like, he saw his warnings go unheeded and he was cashiered from the army, a broken man.

Tiomkin and Webster decided on a narrative ballad form for the

Outside the Kremlin, 1966

With Leopold Stokowski after a screening of Tchaikovsky, *New York, 1972*

title-song with additional verses to link the trial together, a *faux naïf* style to point up the simple morality corrupted and confused in the formal legal process. In the event the ballad was not used for the film, nor was it released as a record. Tiomkin felt that, ironically, he and Webster had succeeded only too well in their self-imposed task and that Billy Mitchell's court-martial was still too controversial a subject to be dealt with openly. The rivalry between the different services of the armed forces was as bitter as it had ever been.

By the late 1960s, Tiomkin was ready for a change. He was growing dissatisfied with the Hollywood scene, which was at that time undergoing one of its periodic phases of radical re-orientation, adjusting itself to the demands of changes in fashion, a new market and a new audience. Tiomkin was jaundiced by the low esteem in which film music seemed to be held within the industry. He was looking out for the kind of film in which the score would be central to the work and not just a decorative afterthought.

The perfect opportunity presented itself with the mammoth Russian-American co-production *Tchaikovsky*. Tiomkin spent several years master-minding this film and it was a project very dear to his heart. The film, which finally saw the light of day in 1971, was fraught with difficulties in its making and indeed at one point Tiomkin found himself personally holding all the English-speaking rights in the film as his American proucers backed out, fearing the picture was turning into a 'filmed LP'. Despite the considerable problems, Tiomkin managed to maintain his native optimism and was proud of his role as a pioneer in the promotion of Russian-American co-productions. *Tchaikovsky* came at a time of growing *entente cordiale* between Russia and the West, when the idea of cultural exchange was an attractive one for both parties.

So, at long last, Tiomkin was finally able to unite his Hollywood-

With Olivia, London, 1972

oriented career with his formal musical upbringing and to see film used to serve the music he loved best. He could scarcely have wished for a more fitting climax and finale to his career as a composer of film music. His life had come full circle and he was once again deeply involved in the music of his homeland, and taking a profound pleasure in the fact that his own artistry was the means of bridging musical, cultural and political divides. Some of his delight in the project was due to the high regard paid to film composers in Russia, in sharp contrast to the treatment he had received in Europe and America. In Russia Tiomkin was able to feel that he had achieved the recognition that his work merited.

After the successful release in Russia and the West of *Tchaikovsky*, Tiomkin undertook no more major projects. Albertina Rasch had died in 1967 and now he felt the time had come to leave Hollywood. He divided his time between Paris, where he took a flat off the Champs Elysées, and London, where he made his home in a secluded residential area. He married his second wife, Olivia Patch, in 1972 and took great pleasure in spending a part of each day in piano practice. He died at home, after a short illness, on 11 November 1979, at the age of eighty-five.

Principal source: *Please Don't Hate Me* (Dimitri Tiomkin and Prosper Buranelli) New York 1959, from which all quotations are taken.

PART II

and tension of those crucial moments are contained in the music which is at this point based mainly on the 'plane' theme — the navigator communicating with the control tower, the gathering excitement as the plane nears land, a burst of orchestral technicolour as the landing lights come on, finally the feeling of exultation as the plane hits the runway and all aboard know they are safe (the cue for which is Wayne's Now I lay me down to sleep'). A great explosion of choral sound marks this moment as the 'High and Mighty' theme returns for its final iteration: Tiomkin like many composers instinctively resorts to voices under the stress of overwhelming emotion.

This unashamed larger-than-lifeness is the essence of Hollywood, and it is no accident that Tiomkin's most enduring claim to fame lies perhaps in his treatment of great Western epics like *Red River* and *Duel in the Sun*. These scores are 'rhetorical' in the non-pejorative sense: they persuade and impress. In a sense, of course, the American West as evoked in his music and as portrayed in the films for which the music was written, never really existed. It was all part of the Hollywood myth, and in this respect we can draw an interesting parallel between Tiomkin's work and that of the late-nineteenth-century artists Frederic Remington and Charles B. Russell. They, like him, viewed the West from an expansively romantic, essentially nineteenth-century viewpoint, and their pictures decisively influenced the ideology and iconography of the Hollywood Western. This is not to suggest, however, that Tiomkin merely perpetuated a received tradition or cliché of commercial Americana. He received this tradition certainly, worked within its bounds, and in his earlier Westerns (*Red River* and *Duel in the Sun*) employed its conventions; but he quickly stamped it with his own distinguishing mark, and later works like *Gunfight at the OK Corral* and *Last Train from Gun Hill* are almost completely lacking in stereotyped Hollywood Americana. After all, he had reason to feel an empathy for the American West. He came from a Big Country too, and in its bigness – particulary its vast all-embracingness of sky and plain — he must have seen a reflection of the steppes of his native Ukraine. So the cowboy becomes a mirror-image of the Cossack: both are primitives and innocents, etched on and dwarfed by a landscape of soul-stirring immensity and rugged masculine beauty. And as an exile himself Tiomkin would doubtless have identified with the cowboys, pioneers and early settlers who people the world of the Western; they like him were itinerants,wanderers in search of a home, in search of money because money brought security in a foreign and as yet untried land where the only law was the survival of the fittest. Those like

Tiomkin who blazed a trail in Hollywood were actually winning the West all over again. This is surely why his Western music has such dynamism and commitment, for in it he is actually reliving a part of his own experience. Prince Sergei Obolensky could easily have been writing of his friend Tiomkin when he described himself as 'one man in his time, simply an ex-Russian of a particular background and family, the foundations of whose existence were destroyed'. Yet for Obolensky, Tiomkin and their like, permanent exile failed to destroy their faith, their interest in the world and their love of life.

It has long been recognized, in fact, that the phenomenon of Hollywood was almost entirely the creation of European expatriates and that few, if any, indigenous American elements were involved. As John Baxter has noted in his book *The Hollywood Exiles*: 'Few ideas or institutions in Los Angeles belong to California . . . the film industry we know as "Hollywood" grew out of foreign ideology. Indigenous American cinema died in the early 1920s, with its best artists destroyed by their own artistic and business naïveté and the growth of a commercial film industry to which they could not adjust — an industry founded and propagated by Europeans.' The case of Hollywood music was no different. Until the early 1950s the stylistic norm remained resolutely that of late-nineteenth-century European romanticism, even when its practitioners were not actually Europeans — which they generally were. Now Tiomkin came from even further afield, from St Petersburg via Berlin, Paris and New York. When he arrived in Hollywood he had had hardly any composing experience, if we discount the numerous songs and piano pieces written in the American popular style of the day, none of which bears any trace of individuality. He had been trained as a pianist, not as a composer, and it remains something of a phenomenon that at the age of forty and more he taught himself what was virtually a completely new trade. The achievement is the more remarkable when one recalls that composing is scarcely an ability that lends itself to being 'picked up' in middle life; if one has a talent in that direction one naturally practises it from a very early age, and it is rare for a composer to be as old as forty before he reaches stylistic maturity. But in Tiomkin's exceptional case he was around forty before he even started, and some sixty years of age before, in the 1950s, he reached the zenith of his compositional powers. (The war years, which he spent for the most part scoring war documentaries, must have arrested his development to a certain extent by virtue of the highly specialized musico-dramatic framework into which they locked him.) We should also remember that he began to conduct his own scores even later, in his fifties. He was the first to admit that by the highest professional standards he wasn't a good conductor — 'I don't enjoy the work as a gifted conductor does,' he wrote, 'I became a conductor in spite of myself, and the job's a chore. I get results by dint of sweat and toil.' The very fact that, at an age when most men have long ceased to be malleable, he was prepared to face and overcome the enormous technical challenges involved in conducting for films, bears witness to that indomitable will-to-succeed which is so often to be noted in men who, like Tiomkin, come from a background of deprivation and instability.

No one starting to compose so late in life can hope to acquire real technical fluency; yet in Tiomkin's case, in an extraordinary way, this was all to the good. It meant that his dramatic sense developed as one of instinct rather than of intellect; he had to rely more on inspiration than on technique. Hence an element of the unconventional and unpredictable: if an idea seemed right for a scene he would implement it, regardless of whether it was the conventional or unconventional thing to do. Highly unconventional is his handling of *Gunfight at the OK Corral*, in which the ballad singer sings throughout the film, summarizing, commenting upon and even anticipating the action in the manner of the chorus in Greek tragedy. The ballad itself is a fine one (though less well known than its predecessor in *High Noon*, a score in which Tiomkin is still groping his way towards the consumma-tion achieved in *Gunfight*) and the tune is the source of virtually every bar of the orchestral music. This gives the film a unique integrity.

Conversely, Tiomkin could take a musical cliché of the most disreputable kind and reinstate it as a meaningful statement — which is what all clichés were before they became mindlessly reiterated as stock formulas. The wonderful unaccompanied choral music behind the scene of the travellers' first sight of the celestial Shangri-La in *Lost Horizon* is not in any way a Hollywoodian 'Heavenly Chorus', simply because it represents Tiomkin's natural, instinctive, spontaneous response to the poetry of the scene. To my mind, the affinity is more with a work like Delius's *Song of the High Hills*, where the wordless choir is also used to convey the related emotions of awe, rapture and ecstasy. To point to the lack of surface polish and elegance in Tiomkin's work, to the absence of any gloss of sophisticated 'correctness', is simultaneously to draw attention to one of its greatest sources of strength, its rough-hewn quality, its quasi-primitive vitality, its earthy peasant-like directness. It can pierce to the core of a dramatic situation with an instinctive, instinctual soundness.

Lillian Gish
Lionel Barrymore
Gregory Peck
Jennifer Jones
Joseph Cotten
Walter Huston
Herbert Marshall

David O. Selznick PRESENTS

"TWO ON THE AISLE"
INSPIRED BY DAVID O. SELZNICK'S
TECHNICOLOR PRODUCTION

DUEL in the SUN

BOSTON "POPS" ORCHESTRA
ARTHUR FIEDLER, CONDUCTOR

PLAYING DIMITRI TIOMKIN SCORE

Art Director . . . . JOHN L. PARVIN
Recording Director . . . . RICHARD GILBERT
Sound Engineer . . . . FRED LYNCH

Duel in the Sun—Front Liner

*The original Arthur Fiedler Boston Pops album
of* Duel in the Sun

Sheet music montage of Rio Bravo

When Tiomkin began to work in films he was naturally forced into the stylistic context already established by Max Steiner *et al.* Not that this was temperamentally uncongenial by any means: Tiomkin was not modernistically minded as a composer, however enterprising his programme as piano recitalist may have been. He stated his own credo unequivocally enough in *Please Don't Hate Me*:

> I take as detached a view of myself as I can. The vogue in highbrow music today is the harsh, atonal school . . . and I'm not in sympathy with it. I've gone over to the technology of motion pictures, music for the masses, music for the machine in an age of machines. Music for movies gives me many opportunities to compose in as fine a style as I am capable of. There's a chance for a fugal passage trimly written, here a rondo; and I can even speak learnedly of a passacaglia in a picture.

But then in 1936 along came *Lost Horizon*, the film whose poetic and visionary qualities served to bring Tiomkin the real composer out of his shell for the first time, disclosing as it did in the Shangri-La scenes a certain genus of musical response which lay without the Hollywood mainstream of the day and which, I feel, may fairly be ascribed to the composer's Russian origins. Most of Tiomkin's work from this time on bears broad signs of a Russian romantic derivation, and much of its abiding interest consists in the fact that these characteristically Russian elements — dormant throughout the long years preceding the start of his composing career — are precisely what lent his style its peculiar distinction and saved it from the anonymity which overwhelmed many of his Hollywood colleagues. Tiomkin's music is indeed profoundly Russian, not so much in the sense of actual reminiscence as in the ways of thinking, feeling and reacting musically that it reveals.

The distinguishing marks of the Russian cast of creative musical mind were first comprehensively tabulated by the English musicologist Gerald Abraham, whose studies of Russian composers, published in the 1930s, have now attained the status of classics. If we turn to his chapters entitled 'The essence of Russian music' in *Studies in Russian Music* and 'Some psychological peculiarities of Russian creative artists' in *On Russian Music*, we find on almost every page meaningful observations as applicable to Tiomkin as to any of the composers Abraham cites to illustrate his points. First – and basically – he finds that most Russian composers prefer to start with a *trouvaille* or *donnée*, a 'given fact', rather than to create in a vacuum. This partially explains the outstanding success of such composers as Tchaikovsky and Stravinsky in ballet, or Prokofiev and Shostakovich in film. The rest of the explanation is to be sought in the plain but vitally determining fact that, in Abraham's words, 'the basis of modern musical construction in Western Europe, the system of logical development of germinal ideas, of which Beethoven was the first really important master, is entirely foreign to the spirit of Russian music. Progressive thinking . . . is not the Russian's way of going about things; his mental process is more akin to brooding, a continual turning over of ideas in his mind, viewing them from different angles, throwing them against strange and fantastic backgrounds, but never *evolving* anything from them . . . he makes the most of his subject by showing it passively in fresh circumstances instead of by setting it in active conflict with something else.' In other words, Russian music does not grow, and even the greatest of Russian operas – Mussorgsky's *Boris Godunov*, Borodin's *Prince Igor*, Prokofiev's *War and Peace* – are more a series of tableaux than a dramtically unfolded action. Abraham concludes 'it is as natural for a Russian to think episodically as for a Frenchman to think logically'. The ability to 'think episodically' is of course an essential qualification for any composer designing to apply himself to film composition; the 'system of logical development of germinal ideas' is as foreign to the nature of film music as it is to the spirit of Russian music, there being neither the time nor the opportunity. So we can see already that the process of film composing is well enough suited to the Russian creative temperament. And when Abraham describes Russian composers as not developing but continually *modifying* their material, viewing their ideas from different angles, 'throwing them against strange and fantastic backgrounds', he could easily have in mind a number of the finest moments in Tiomkin's work, for all of which this repetition-with-modification principle is responsible: the *Lost Horizon* funeral cortège, 'Pharaoh's Procession' in *Land of the Pharaohs*, the magnificent 'Pax Romana' sequence in *The Fall of the Roman Empire*. All these processional movements are brilliantly cumulative in effect, but colouristically and two-dimensionally so, not symphonically. The monothematic structure of *High Noon* and *Gunfight at the OK Corral* also falls into this category: the idea of basing an entire score on a single theme could scarcely be put successfully into practice were a typically Russian resourcefulness in repetition-with-modification not to replace the process of symphonic evolution for which the film-score framework offers insufficient scope.

In the light of this all-important characteristic it becomes easy to understand the attraction folksong has always held for Russian composers from Glinka on; for folksong, being already a full developed whole, contains no growing power: it can therefore be varied and modified *ad infinitum*, but not symphonically treated in any positive way. Tiomkin's response to his native folk music resembles that of Rimsky-Korsakov and Glazunov under whose aegis he grew up, inasmuch as he absorbed it sufficiently to result in his thinking melodically on occasion in an identifiably Russian manner even when there is no exterior justification. Russian folksong inflections, cadences and turns of melodic phrase turn up with tolerable frequency in his scores, even whole melodies of a distinctly Russian profile, such as the theme of the barbarians' devastations in *The Fall of the Roman Empire*:

Most explicit of all is the second strain of the *Guns of Navarone* main theme, with its *Volga Boatmen*-like interval of the falling fourth:

One wonders, too, whether the wordless choral music which marks the first sight of the Celestial City in *Lost Horizon* would possess the magic it does without some dim recollection on Tiomkin's part of the chant of the Russian Orthodox Church. However, it may be felt that Tiomkin's partial folksong orientation proved most greatly of value in that it enabled him to acquire elements of other folk cultures as and when they proved dramatically necessary. I'm thinking mainly of course of his handling of the American folk idiom in such films as *Giant*, *The Big Sky*, *Mr Smith goes to Washington*, *Canadian Pacific* and others; two classic non-American examples are the Iberian fishermen's scenes of early-morning departure and return off the coast of Cuba in *The Old Man and the Sea* (male choir *a cappella*) and the extraordinary measureless theme in *Lost Horizon* which has something of the 'continuous continuation' of true oriental music. It is perhaps too not without significance that *Lost Horizon*, which represents the first real milestone in Tiomkin's career as a composer, should be a picture with an oriental setting. Exoticism has always bulked larger in the work of Russian composers than in that of their Western contemporaries (after all, the kind of glamorous fairy-tale musical orientalism which served Hollywood so well was basically the creation of Rimsky-Korsakov, following in the wake of Glinka and Balakirev). Later Tiomkin scores in which an important exotic element is present include *Land of the Pharaohs*, *Search for Paradise* and *55 Days at Peking* — the opening of the overture to which is for me the epitome of the Tartar spirit in music.

The same taste for sugar and spice is reflected in the Russians' love of bright primary orchestral colours, and a recurring feature of Tiomkin's orchestrations is their spectacular colourfulness; his is almost a pure childlike delight in sound for its own sake. (This, of course, is also a characteristic of French Impressionism and goes some of the way towards explaining the oft-remarked Franco-Russian *entente cordiale*. Impressionistic tendencies in Tiomkin's work are particularly notice-able in *Search for Paradise*, *Tarzan and the Mermaids* and *The Old Man and the Sea*; and *Portrait of Jennie* is based almost entirely on music by Debussy.)

Gerald Abraham has also pointed out that in more purely musical matters such as counterpoint the working of the Russian mind differs essentially from that of the Western:

> Genuine contrapuntal feeling, the natural flowing together of parallel, simultaneous streams of thought, is practically unknown in Russian music. On the other hand, some of the Russians have been very fond of using contrapuntal means in constructing their music, a fundamentally different matter. Borodin, in particular, frequently shows great ingenuity in juggling with combinations of themes, but the themes (as in the well-known *In the Steppes of Central Asia*) are only *fitted* together; they have not *grown* together. There is nothing forced or unnatural about the fitting.

For 'Borodin' in the latter part of this quotation substitute 'Tiomkin', for this process of contrapuntal dovetailing of themes is one of his fingerprints. Sometimes whole distinct themes are worked together, as in the *Lost Horizon* finale; the *Search for Paradise* epilogue at one point combines 'Happy land of Hunza' in the brass with the baritone soloist's 'Somewhere in the distance' (the main theme). Elsewhere the two complementary strains of a single theme are fitted together, as in the *Land of the Pharaohs* finale, the poetic *pianissimo* choral epilogue to *The Guns of Navarone*, and at the climax of 'Pax Romana' in *The*

Fall of the Roman Empire. Yet again, in some cases themes which have essentially nothing whatever to do with each other are brought together for special dramatic effect: as for instance when 'Happy land of Hunza' is superimposed on the wild native dance in 'Bucephalus ritual' (*Search for Paradise*) or the moment in *The Fall of the Roman Empire* when the Neapolitan tarantella becomes gradually overwhelmed by the 'Fall of Rome' theme in heavy brass and organ. Most effective of all, perhaps, is the merging of the 'Western' and 'Eastern' themes during the Lama's funeral cortège in *Lost Horizon* at the moment when Conway is forced to flee the valley.

On a more general level Abraham observes that 'perhaps the most valuable of all the qualities of Russian music is its compressed force and directness of expression... the Russians have always been remarkable for their pointed, forceful brevity'. The ability to write with 'compressed force and directness of expression' is, of course, a valuable asset for a film composer, the nature of whose medium is necessarily opposed to prolixity. To be sure, Tiomkin is no miniaturist and prefers to fill a large canvas, but actual size has nothing to do with it; rather is the nature and quality of the thought expressed the point at issue. By way of pointed, forceful brevity, Tiomkin frequently comes up with short and pithy musical sayings the impact of which is like a blow straight from the shoulder and *ipso facto* effective dramatically — as for instance the parachutists' motif in the *Search for Paradise* prologue:

Closely akin to this is the famous Russian *realism*. To quote Abraham:

> The most superficial student of Russian literature knows that its predominant note is realism: the tendency, that is, to start from a basis of given facts and, broadly speaking, to portray them closely and accurately. The music of Dargomizhsky and Mussorgsky, which had next to nothing in common with Wagner's, was a sort of literal translation of words and even gestures into tones, a type of music very close to its verbal or pantomimic *donné.*

Now is this realism not the nub of Tiomkin's thought again and again — the 'basis of given facts' being the motion picture scenario, the task he sets himself the 'literal translation' of its action into tones? Two examples immediately spring to mind, both from *Land of the Pharaohs*. 'The building of the tomb' is conceived with a quasi-operatic realism, the mainspring of the musical action being the singing of the myriad workers engaged in constructing the pyramid; the rhythmic sound of hammering and chiselling is also incorporated in the orchestral texture. And in 'The sealing of the tomb' Tiomkin's main business is to reinforce the physical sound of the pouring sand which inexorably forces the stones into immovable position. The cartoon documentary *Rhapsody of Steel* demands and receives a consistent realism of musical treatment, and this little-known score must surely be accounted one of Tiomkin's finest achievements. In this connection also Abraham remarks that 'the excitement which Russian music manifests... is almost always physical, a direct glorification of the animal joy of living.' Do we not owe to this the particular kind of bustling energy and hectic exuberance which must rank as one of Tiomkin's most readily recognizable characteristics? In this connection we should bear in mind his early experiences as pianist for his wife's ballet troupe. The peculiar electricity and nervosity demonstrated by (to quote three examples among hundreds) the chase music in *D.O.A.*, the tennis game in *Strangers on a Train* and the ambulance-call at the beginning of *Angel Face* suggest a balletic origin, as does the quite choreographic approach adopted to the showdown scenes in *Red River, High Noon* and *Gunfight at the OK Corral*.

Abraham concedes, however, that there are certain areas of expression in which the Russian composer is notably deficient: 'Hardly any of the best Russian music is inspired by erotic emotion... and when Russian composers are unable to scamp the love-interest altogether, they generally provide it perfunctorily.' Abraham goes on to point out that, on the credit side, 'a quick reaction to any suggestion of the grotesque is noticeable' (*Cyrano de Bergerac*) and that all Russian composers show a penchant for the romantic (in the widest sense) and the heroic; such excellent scores as *Lost Horizon, The Alamo, The Old Man and the Sea, Search for Paradise* and *The Fall of the Roman Empire* obviously qualify for inclusion here.

Finally we may note a curious parallel between Tiomkin and such Russian artists as Gogol, Tolstoy, Balakirev and Rimsky-Korsakov, namely their tendency to stop and change direction in mid-career. It is perhaps not a very valid parallel inasmuch as Tiomkin's change from concert pianist to film composer was brought about by material circumstances, not through any kind of inner crisis. But we should also bear in mind that before Rimsky-Korsakov was a composer he was a naval officer; that Mussorgsky was originally in the army; and that Borodin was a professional chemist as well as a spare-time composer. Balakirev, the focal point of the nationalist circle to which they all belonged, was almost entirely self-taught. It has been plausibly suggested that much of their vitality and originality was due to their lack of any rigorous formal training during what are conventionally thought of as formative years. Could, I wonder, a similar case be made out for Tiomkin?

In any event, the way in which Tiomkin encompassed this change-in-direction and turned all its circumstances to his own advantage was typical of his natural shrewdness and adaptability: qualities which enabled him to survive in revolution-torn St Petersburg, in inflation-ravaged Berlin and — in many respects the most daunting of all — in the cut-throat competitive community of Hollywood. His years as a 'Vaudevillian' not only developed his sense of what was theatrically effective; they also, on his own admission, trained him to gauge the popular temper and taste of the times and to supply the need of the moment. For no other composer in Hollywood managed so successfully to combine the sincerity of the composer who provides music as an adjunct to drama with the showmanship of the entertainer who woos his audience with irresistible melodies. The result of these combined assets was not only a more widespread publicity than any other Hollywood composer of the day received, but also a vaster fortune. Yet we need look no further than *The Men* for a fine example of the warmth and intensity of Tiomkin's musical response to an emotional crux. Here Marlon Brando plays a young paraplegic who, after a violent paroxysm of resentment and bitterness, determines all at once to come to terms with his life again. Music is introduced (for the second time only since the beginning of the film) as he reaches agonizingly upwards for the strap-handles and, whilst being intricately co-ordinated with the rhythmic montage of rehabilitation exercises which follows, movingly expresses the surge and throb of new-found optimism.

The Tiomkin treasure-trove of songs is vast. As we know he practised the craft of popular song-writing assiduously during the 1920s and 1930s, and though few of these efforts found their way into print at this stage of his career, a number resurfaced in later years in a motion-picture context. (One such was the main theme of Hitchcock's *I Confess*, here provided with the new lyric of 'Love, look what you've done to me'.) After the success of *High Noon* in 1952 Tiomkin formed what amounted to a regular song-writing partnership with both Ned Washington and Paul Frances Webster,* and melodies from almost every film score he produced thereafter were extracted and fitted with words by the one or the other. 'Rawhide' (from the television series of the same name), 'Thee I love' from *Friendly persuasion,*** 'Do not forsake me' from *High Noon*, 'The green leaves of summer, and 'Ballad of the Alamo' from *The Alamo* have virtually passed into Americana; scarcely less well known are 'Giant, 'The High and the Mighty', 'Town without Pity', 'Return to Paradise', 'Wild is the Wind', all from the films of the same name. As is the capricious way of things, equally good songs which failed to become hits include 'Quand je rêve' (*The Big Sky*), 'Wait for love' from *Tension at Table Rock*, 'Nostalgia' from *Angel Face* and 'So little time' from *55 Days at Peking*. *The Guns of Navarone* features two expert Kurt Weill pastiches to German words by Alfred Perry: 'Treu sein' and 'Das Sundenlied'. The soundtrack never gave them a chance to become popular since they are heard merely as source music on a distant radio during the scenes immediately preceding the storming of the fortress. Even less chance was given the exhilarating 'It's a wonderful life' (lyric by Frederick Herbert) inasmuch as the song was never incorporated in the film of the same name at all, thus sharing the fate of much of the incidental music written by Tiomkin for this film and arbitrarily discarded by the director. A similar case was the ballad written for Otto Preminger's *Court Martial of Billy Mitchell* which never reached the scoring stage. Many attractive songs originated in films which have not stood the test of time, like the cowboy ballad 'Follow the river' from *Night Passage*, the three songs in *Search for*

*Tiomkin was a loyal man as far as professional colleagues were concerned. His team of orchestral arrangers and assistants (chief among them Manuel Emanuel, George Parrish, Paul Marquardt, Herb Taylor and David Tamkin) remained much the same from the late 1930s to the end of his career; he employed Jester Hairston as choral director/arranger on most of his films after *Lost Horizon* in which chorus was involved, often in the teeth of studio administrative opposition rooted in colour prejudice; and from the late 1940s on his favourite music editor was Richard (Dick) Harris. He had been impressed by the latter's skill in assembling the soundtrack of *It's a Wonderful Life*, even though this had involved the cutting of much of Tiomkin's own music *out* and the cutting of other people's *in*!

**Friendly Persuasion* yielded a whole crop of charming songs in addition to 'Thee I love' — 'Marry me', 'Lead her like a pigeon', 'The mockingbird in the willow tree', 'Coax me a little' and the polka 'Indiana holiday'.

Paradise (see p.113), 'Strange are the ways of love' from *The Young Land*, 'Happy time' from the film of the same name, 'If you're in love' from *The Fourposter* and 'I feel wonderful' from *Rhapsody of Steel*. Mention should also be made of the catchy march from *Champion* which became popular as an instrumental selection, and of the graceful *Prince and Princess Waltz* written for the wedding of Princess Grace and Prince Rainier of Monaco – one of the few Tiomkin songs *not* specifically written for a motion picture.

Tiomkin's counterpart in the realm of conducting may well be Leopold Stokowski, for both men demonstrated that seriousness of purpose need not be incompatible with catering to the needs of a majority audience. Certainly no composer of symphonic film music has hit the popular jackpot as often as Tiomkin: in fact, to many he must be far better known as a composer of song hits than of 'serious' film music. Whilst it is true that the phenomenal success of 'Do not forsake me', played, hummed and sung throughout *High Noon*, encouraged producers in the belief that the prime function of film music was to boost the financial returns of a picture, in *High Noon* itself the song *as* a song was conceived as an integral part of the score; and though many of Tiomkin's later pictures had songs with lyrics associated with them, the melody was always built into the score first, *then* extracted and fitted with lyrics. And when lyrics are heard on the soundtrack they may well be relevant to the action on the screen — as with the justly celebrated 'Green leaves of summer' and 'Tennessee babe', both of which are heard sung *pianissimo* by unaccompanied chorus in the closing stages of *The Alamo* (1960). Here, as in *The Guns of Navarone* finale which also featured the *pianissimo* chorus, Tiomkin managed to do what he had often attempted in the early days but had always been overruled — end a picture on a 'dying fall'.

Magnificently as he handled the epic — and incomparably as it was enhanced by the colourful grandiloquence of his style — it should not be overlooked that he was also capable of effects of delicacy and subtlety. The Hollywood convention was that every film should open and close in a blare and blaze of sound, regardless of its dramatic appropriateness. Yet *55 Days at Peking* — Bronston's multi-million dollar reconstruction of the Boxer Rebellion — opens with the serenity of muted strings playing one of Tiomkin's tenderest melodies; and a Western epic, *The Big Sky*, begins and ends *pianissimo* with music reflecting the majesty and beauty of the Missouri riverscape, an omnipresent feature of the film.

Tiomkin's film scores embrace an extraordinarily wide stylistic range,

and one which is done scant justice by his prevailing reputation as a
'heavyweight'. It is a far cry from the beguiling intimacies of *Friendly
Persuasion* to the racy effervescence of *The Happy Time, Champagne
for Caesar* or *The Fourposter* with its interpolated UPA cartoons; from
the *alfresco* magnificence of prairie and river as evoked in *The Big
Sky* or *Canadian Pacific* to the claustrophobic big-city nightmare of
D.O.A.; from the rampant, extravagant exoticism of *55 Days at
Peking* to the spare, clipped, piano-dominated sonorities of *36 Hours*;
from the tense interior drama of *I Confess* to the drily witty quasi-
neoclassicism of *Cyrano de Bergerac*; from the sustained symphonic
hysteria of *The Steel Trap* or *The Well* to the jazz-inflected emotion
of *Town Without Pity*; from the intimidating atmospherics of *The
Thing* to the sunny, folksy innocence of *The Sundowners*; from the
gaudy swashbucklery of *Hajji Baba* to the Disney-like picturesqueness
of *Tarzan and the Mermaids*; from the blustering jingoism of *Take the
High Ground* to the compassionate commitment of *The Men*; from
the ardent romanticism of *Wild is the Wind* to the sharp-featured,
neon-lit cynicism of *Champion*; yet everything bears the stamp of his
unique and inimitable personality. Tiomkin had a knowledge and
understanding of the film medium that few could rival. He was grateful
to the cinema for offering him a positive and viable outlet for his
composing talent and allowing him to write in as fine a style as he
was capable of; and in return he left his mark on other aspects apart
from the purely musical of the films with which he was associated.
One distinguished director has described him as 'the finest film-editor
I know; and through collaborating and working intimately with him I
had the sense of my eyes and ears being opened for the first time'.
The day would have obviously come when Tiomkin would take charge
of a film of his own; and his chance came in the 1960s when the
post-Stalinist 'thaw' enabled him to realize his lifelong ambition to
shoot, produce and score a film biography of Tchaikovsky in Russian,
in Russia. For a composer who, as man and artist, never (as I have
tried to show) relinquished or gainsaid his specifically Russian identity,
it was a fitting swansong.

PART III

Landmarks

Lost Horizon (1937)

*Lost Horizon** was Tiomkin's first score of substance and the one which raised him to the forefront of Hollywood composers. Capra in his autobiography wrote of the finished film: 'Curiosity had forced me to sneak unseen into the music scoring stage to overhear Steiner's first orchestral rehearsal of the main-title music. I left with stars in my eyes. Tiomkin's music not only captured the mood, but darned near captured the film.' He had wanted Tiomkin on the set during the shooting of the film, which took five months (excluding some retakes and scenes added later), and during this time, from June or July 1936 on, Tiomkin actually composed much of the music heard in the finished score. It seems that the actual tailoring of the music to the assembled film began with a version which ran approximately 30 reels, since, for example, the music for the funeral procession of the High Lama is marked 'Reel 26', and the film would probably have run four (or more) reels longer. Using nine and a half minutes as an average running time of a reel, such a version would have run for over five hours. This more or less corresponds with information given to the press that Capra would be (as of 29 October 1936) reducing 30,000 feet of negative footage (about six hours) to 12,000 feet (about two and a half hours). So it seems reasonable to assume that Tiomkin was fitting the music to a rough-cut of the film. If we compare the descriptions of action and timings on Tiomkin's sketches with the final shooting script, it looks very much as though the composer wrote music for most of this five-hour version of the film! However, at least half of this music was

*The rather chequered history of its composition has been scrupulously researched by William H. Rosar, from whose article 'Lost Horizon – an account of the composition of the score' (published in Elmer Bernstéin's *Film Music Notebook*, vol. IV, 1978) many of the facts and documentation set forth here are taken.

not orchestrated and never reached the scoring stage, since the film subsequently underwent drastic cutting and changes. As these cuts were made, Tiomkin was furnished with new timing breakdowns so that he could cut and adjust his music to correspond with the running times.

Max Steiner was borrowed from Warner Brothers to supervise and conduct Tiomkin's score. (At this early stage Tiomkin had not yet learned how to conduct and was still relatively inexperienced generally at fitting music to timed sequences.) Of his working relationship with Steiner, Tiomkin recalls in *Please Don't Hate Me*:

> *Lost Horizon* spoiled me completely. The conductor was Max Steiner, who was also a first-rate composer. Composers are usually jealous of each other, like rival tenors in an opera company; but Steiner had only one idea — to get the best out of the score. If I made a suggestion, he wanted to find out what was in my mind and do it that way. He was responsible for much of the musical success of the film.

The orchestra used to record the score was enormous by Hollywood standards of those days. Ranging from about forty-five to sixty-five pieces, it incorporated a large battery of percussion instruments, and in addition the Hall Johnson Choir, a very popular group of Negro singers, was featured in certain sequences. Juilliard-trained composer-arranger Jester Hairston, then a member of the Choir, made the choral arrangements. (Hairston was later associated with Tiomkin on such scores as *Portrait of Jennie*, *Duel in the Sun*, *Land of the Pharaohs*, etc.) As had become customary, the chorus was recorded separately and was mixed in later, although according to Steiner the two ensembles were rehearsed together.

Columbia released a publicity sheet (presumably just prior to the recording of the score) which was titled 'A Picture for the Classroom'. Of the music it stated:

> A musical score, which includes authentic folk songs of Tibet, has been arranged by Dimitri Tiomkin.
>
> For the recording, Max Steiner will conduct an orchestra of sixty pieces, many of which are Tibetan instruments never before used in America.
>
> The Hall Johnson Choir will sing the folk song arrangements in the native Tibetan language. One of particular interest is that sung during the funeral procession of the High Lama.

Tiomkin with Henry Eichheim examining the latter's unique collection of oriental instruments

In retrospect this sounds rather like studio 'hype', since although oriental instruments did in fact appear in the picture (loaned to the studio by the Santa Barbara composer Henry Eichheim), they were not actually heard. It is not impossible that Tiomkin had originally wanted Eichheim's instruments to be heard in the score (as numerous press stories would seem to suggest) but that this idea was ultimately abandoned in favour of a conventional orchestra. An obvious reason why the instruments could not be used as part of the orchestration would be the problem of finding people to play them! Photographs taken in July 1936 show Tiomkin with Eichheim in Eichheim's music room at his home in Santa Barbara surrounded by the oriental instruments. Eichheim was an authority on eastern music, and it seems more than likely that Tiomkin consulted him on Tibetan music while there. Certainly there are some peculiarities about the main *Lost Horizon* theme which make one wonder if Tiomkin might not have drawn on elements of authentic eastern music in composing it. If so, it was a procedure he would resort to again in scores such as *Spawn of the North* (1938) and *The Old Man and the Sea* (1958).

Recording of the score began on 23 October 1936 and continued until 29 October. In this time eight major sequences were recorded, and correlating them with the timing sheets prepared for the preview of the film suggests that it was with this music alone that the film was previewed. Max Steiner recalled certain details of the final preparation of the score for the recording:

> During the scoring of this picture we had to do quite a lot of revising. Capra kept on changing the picture, and so I used to revise whatever was required during the daytime. Then we would start to record about eight o'clock at night and seldom finish until six or seven in the morning.

Capra writes that the film had been a complete success at private studio screenings, and that he was utterly bewildered by the audience's hostile reaction at the preview in Santa Barbara. Major cuts were made, and Tiomkin resumed work on the score. Sequences that had been composed but not recorded for the Santa Barbara preview were revised and orchestrated, while sequences that were in the preview version were modified. Even as late as 20 January 1937 the film was still not finished, and it was not until 1 February that recording of the score began again.

The film was premiered on 19 February and this time the favourable response of the public and critics alike was unanimous. More than one trade paper mentioned the music, a none-too-common occurrence. In *Please Don't Hate Me* Tiomkin recalled the response of one famous musician to his score:

> At the Hollywood première of the picture I met George Gershwin going into the theatre. 'They tell me, Dimi, you have something special here,' he said. He spoke with his usual smiling courtesy, but I thought I detected an amused scepticism – the Russian pianist

Sheet music montage of I Confess

Giant *poster*

Lost Horizon - *Capra, Ronald Colman and Tiomkin*

who played Gershwin jazz at the Paris Opéra now a composer for Hollywood films.

During the picture I sat just behind him, and soon he turned, nodded, and gave the Broadway-Hollywood sign of excellence – thumb and forefinger making a circle. That, I felt, was tops in criticism.

The suite derived from the score was performed at the Hollywood Bowl, on 16 August 1938, with the composer conducting the Los Angeles Philharmonic Orchestra and the Hall Johnson Choir. This was in fact the first time he conducted in public.

The James Hilton novel tells of a plane hijacked while flying from revolution-torn China and taken with its passengers over uncharted areas of the Himalayas to the paradisial valley of Shangri-La where the inhabitants have discovered the secret of quasi-perpetual youth. West meets East and is ennobled and transfigured by the encounter; with the exception of Robert Conway's brother George, all the occupants of the hijacked plane find lasting peace and contentment in the Tibetan community. This dichotomy is cleverly mirrored in the structure of the two main musical themes of the picture. The first represents the harassed world-weary West and is a stylized Hollywood love-theme such as might have come from many another hand of the period. The second theme is an extraordinary, if not unique, inspiration. The written score has bar lines, but they mean nothing; strong and weak beats, metric definition, conventional Western phrase structure that involves one phrase ending and another beginning — all are absent; should we try to phrase the melody, the phrase mark would never come to an end. Rather there is an affinity with oriental or medieval monody in which tune is never-ending; it just flows on and on, perpetually regenerating itself — the 'continuous continuation' of the Orient as opposed to the Western concept of 'moment in time'. There is no 'stress' here (in the technical, musical sense) just as there is no 'stress' (in the wider, general sense) in the Valley of the Blue Moon; we have in fact the ageless beauty and serenity of Shangri-La in a musical nutshell: immortality, lux perpetua. Anything further removed from the tradition of trumpery Chu-Chin-Chow-like confection that so often in Hollywood does duty for the Orient would be hard to imagine. The pull and thrust between these two disparate thematic entities complements the conflict on the screen, most skilfully in the scene of the funeral procession of the High Lama. Here the 'Eastern' theme is given to the mixed chorus keening wordlessly over the persistent funereal thudding of the timpani; the orchestral texture incorporates a

variety of exotic percussion, metallophones, gongs, xylophones and
bells redolent of the Javanese gamelan or percussion orchestra. The
procession files endlessly up the hill to the lamasery, torches flicker
round the courts and pavilions, the musicians blow and beat, the
keening voices fade on a veer of the wind, returning to fade again.
But at this very moment of the Lama's obsequies Conway is persuaded
by his brother to flee the valley, and is pursued by Sondra. This posed
a problem, since the 'on-stage' music of the cortège had in some way
to be reconciled with the dramatic music required by the new turn of
events. An easy solution would have been artificially to fade the one
down and the other up, but Tiomkin's masterly solution is to build the
love theme contrapuntally into the cortège and write the overlap
directly into the music. As the sound of the cortège — the 'Eastern'
theme — is lost in the distance, the 'western' love theme gains in
ascendancy and comes into full focus, raging desperately as Sondra
reaches the entrance and looks out helplessly after the disappearing
party. Ultimately Conway finds his way back to his lost paradise, and
the finale, resplendent with bells and chimes, is a *grandioso* restatement
of the 'Eastern' Shangri-La theme, pealed out on the full orchestra as
Conway stands erect, eyes shining, once more at the entrance to the
celestial Valley of the Blue Moon.

We might reasonably have expected that the 'Eastern' theme would
first emerge *in toto* at the climactic moment when the travellers first
stumble upon the entrance to the Valley. (Incidentally it is worth
remarking the careful timing of the chorus's entry during the main-title
statement of the theme: the voices join in not at the beginning but
only half-way through, to fine effect.) But here, as so often elsewhere,
Tiomkin fails to do the anticipated thing. In the immediately preceding
scenes, music has reflected the melancholy and inertia of the kidnapped
passengers now somewhere on the vast Tibetan plateau, the loftiest
and least hospitable part of the earth's surface. Then dour, nasal
woodwinds — imitating their primitive prototypes — announce the
arrival of Chang (H. B. Warner) and the caravan that escorts the party
on the long trek across the stormswept mountain country to the secret
crevice that alone gives admittance to the Valley of the Blue Moon.
A ponderous march movement builds itself up with Mussorgskian
massiveness, the many 'wrong' notes serving to emphasize something
of the strangeness of the journey, so far removed in its purpose from
the normal range of human experience. A huge climax is reached, but
the music suddenly evaporates; only the chiming of monastery bells is
heard in the distance, for the travellers have come in sight of the

Celestial City. And here, as Conway looks on the clear, sunlit valley, a myriad voices sound from afar. The sound of massed voices singing or murmuring wordlessly in the distance has a mystical quality that almost defies analysis. When used, as here, in its rightful context it seems to stand simply as a symbol of ecstasy, if by ecstasy we understand rapture, wonder, mystery, a withdrawal from the common life and common consiousness – these are the kindred emotions pervading Conway's soul, and through the medium of this choral sequence Tiomkin gives them expression in music. Here is the essence of Shangri-La, 'an earthly paradise whose walls are splayed with centuries-old vines flaunting their fragrant blossoms; whose broad stairway beckons to the great portico of the lamasery; whose acres of flat white roofs shimmer in the sun; where voices are as murmurous as the hum of insects in summer, and rainbow-haloed fountains splash and tinkle in harmony with the evanescent aerial music of circling white doves – a cloistered Eden where people live to unheard-of ages, sedated by a wondrous herb, observing a sunset as men in the outer world hear the striking of a clock, and with much less care, and where art, culture and accumulated knowledge of the world are treasured against the day when civilization will be torn asunder by mechanized warfare on a global scale.' (Capra). Near the end of this scene voices and bells are raised in a chant based on the Chinese pentatonic or five-note scale (it has already been heard once *fortissimo* at the climax of the caravan sequence), which, like the main Shangri-la theme, conforms to no Western standards of metrical regularity; it has rather the cold and tranquil beauty of ancient Chinese lacquers or pearl-blue Sung ceramics. It is heard again exquisitely set as a nocturne during which Conway tries to explain to his brother the strange feeling of fulfilment he experienced upon first encountering the valley; and a particularly felicitous touch is its appearance on the celesta to mark the end of Conway's first interview with the High Lama. Somehow the effect of conventional Hollywoodian Orientalism is consistently negated.

Duel in the Sun (1947)

If *Giant* was to be a kind of Texan *War and Peace, Duel in the Sun* was an attempt on the part of David O. Selznick to make a Texan *Gone with the Wind*. However it was Selznick's policy to involve himself extensively and often intrusively in all aspects of his productions, not least the musical. Tiomkin liked to tell the story of his efforts to

Recording Duel in the Sun *with Jennifer Jones and Gregory Peck on the screen*

find a love-theme (for Jennifer Jones and Gregory Peck) passionate enough to satisfy the producer, but in fact the musical issue was considerably more complicated; very few areas remain in the score that were not at some point subjected to major revisions, either because Selznick did not like them as they were originally — for instance, it is easy to sense Selznick's hand at work in the interminable repetitions of Stephen Foster's 'Beautiful Dreamer' in the scenes at Paradise Flats — or because the picture was re-cut after the music had been composed. Nonetheless, inasmuch as it was the first of his great

Western epics, the score was a landmark in its composer's career. The prelude is a blasting and blistering evocation of the Texan cowboy country with all its heat, noise, dust and sheer intimidating magnificence. It is launched by a broad, lyrical theme associated in the picture with Jennifer Jones and Joseph Cotton (borrowed, incidentally, from Tiomkin's 1941 score for Capra's *Meet John Doe*) and leads into a fiery fanfare-studded *allegro maestoso* in which is presented the main theme (which, interestingly, was conceived many years before in a much slower tempo for a quite different dramatic purpose in another Capra film – for the caravan scene in *Lost Horizon*). There follows music which is melodramatic in the strict sense: designed as accompaniment to the spoken word, in this case the voice of Orson Welles:

> Deep among the sun-baked hills of Texas the great weatherbeaten stone still stands. The Comanches call it Squaw's Head Rock. Time cannot change its impassive face, nor dim the legend of the wild young lovers who found heaven and hell in the shadows of the rock. And this is what the legend says: 'A flower known nowhere else grows from out of the desperate crags where Pearl vanished. Pearl . . ! who was herself a wildflower, sprung from the hard clay: quick to blossom, and early to die.'

The music (making subtle and evocative use of the wordless chorus) turns the words into poetry, setting forth as it does so the themes of the desert and of Pearl Chavez (Jennifer Jones) which are to play the dominant roles in the picture's dénouement Pearl's and Lewt McCanles's (Gregory Peck) rendezvous at Squaw's Head Rock which has fatal consequences for both: they shoot each other, then die in each other's arms. This final sequence opens with the sight and sense of the desert conjured up on stark harmonies, shrill, hoarse woodwind figures, a heavy grinding *basso ostinato;* wordless men's voices add a strange primitive element of unhumanness. The emotional stance changes abruptly after the shooting: the music surges in a perfervid, tumultuous, Skryabinesque development of the love-theme, its heated, impassioned character already established in earlier love-scenes. (It comes as some thing of a surprise to discover this selfsame theme lending itself so naturally to a piquant, scherzo-like transformation for a springtime scene of frolicking colts; and it is also heard, in an arrangement for four solo guitars, as a serenade, i.e., a piece of quasi-source music.) Skryabin incidentally was a Wagnerian whose music is impregnated with a mystico-erotic emotionalism deriving ultimately from *Tristan und Isolde*, and Charles Higham has described *Duel in the*

Sun as a 'Wagnerian horse-opera, a *Liebestod* among the cactus.' Pearl, herself mortally wounded and bleeding profusely, drags herself slowly and painfully under the scorching Texas sun in a frantic attempt to reach the dying Lewt for one final embrace. Tiomkin's music sets out to squeeze every last drop of emotional tension from the situation: the full orchestra develops the tortuous, tortured love-theme to a pitch of almost terrifying intensity, and the climax, when it comes, represents the supreme final ecstasy, the love-in-death. This scene, musically and dramatically, seems on paper to represent the romantic cinema at its hammiest and most cliché-ridden. In the cinema it has the power to move a modern audience profoundly, and it would be a rash critic who would seek to disallow Tiomkin's share of the credit.

The neo-Wagnerian extravaganza of this finale demanded a corresponding degree of stylization in the music; different forms of stylization are encountered also in the 'Western' music (the buggy-ride) and in the Mexican scenes (the children's 'El Bailero' and Pearl's Casino Dance). The latter piece, incidentally (like the riotous 'Fiesta' in another Tiomkin Texan Western, *Strange Lady in Town*) originated as one of the composer's numerous contributions to the repertoire of the Albertina Rasch Dancers.

Duel in the Sun marks Tiomkin out above all as a composer who is not afraid to take the centre of the stage and make a strong, direct, meaningful statement; he refuses point-blank to stand in the wings fumbling with his hat. (In this he is notably unlike many of his present-day colleagues in film.) He is prepared to take thereby the risk of overstepping the bound of conventional 'good taste'; like most artists of his generation and outlook he would prefer to be indicted for sins of commission rather than omission.

The John Wayne Trilogy: Red River (1948) Rio Bravo (1958) The Alamo (1960)

Three John Wayne Westerns for which Tiomkin wrote music together form a trilogy of epic proportions further unified by some interesting musical cross-references. Another common factor is that *Red River* and *Rio Bravo* were both directed by Howard Hawks, with whom Tiomkin otherwise had a particularly fruitful creative relationship (*Only Angels have Wings*, *The Big Sky*, *The Thing* and *Land of the Pharaohs*).

Red River is an epic telling of the men who made the first cattle drive up the Chisholm Trail from Texas to Kansas under the leadership of Tom Dunson (John Wayne), and the title-music immediately sets the epic, heroic tone. The unison horn-call is indeed an invocation: the gates of history are flung wide and the main theme, high and wide as the huge vault of the sky, rides forth in full choral-orchestral splendour (the arrangements for male choir were the work of Jester Hairston, composer of *Mary's Boy Child*, choral trainer and arranger, and one of Tiomkin's most valued associates). The oft-recurring 'cattle' theme (horns again) leads directly into the scenes of departure and the start of the drive. The clip-clop of hooves is heard, and a stray banjo strums to the tune of 'O Susanna'. Stephen Foster also seems to haunt the more lyrical, expressive turn the music takes as Dunson bids an emotional farewell to his sweetheart Fen (Coleen Gray).

The crossing of Red River itself is made to music of a crude, pioneer vitality. Based on a ponderous rhythmic transformation of the 'cattle' theme (which incidentally, like so much 'primitive' and 'innocent' music, is contained within the five-note or pentatonic scale) it suggests grit, energy, determination and the sheer weight of physical effort involved in negotiating a mighty river with an outsize herd of cattle. (Tiomkin even builds the *sound* of the animals, their long-note lowing, into his scoring for brass.) The climax — the great feat accomplished — strikes an exultant note as the main 'Red River' theme (strings) is superimposed contrapuntally on the 'cattle theme' (brass).

The picture's climax is reached in the long-awaited confrontation between Dunson and Matt (Montgomery Clift). The theme of revenge is sounded ominously in the horns and gathers momentum through persistently accelerating repetitions as the music assumes a march-like character; the scene is conceived musically in quasi-choreographic terms and is one of those which may well refer back to the composer's pre-Hollywood involvement in the ballet world.

In *Rio Bravo* the *Red River* main theme is fitted to a new lyric ('My rifle, my pony, and me') and sung in the film during a natural break in the action by Ricky Nelson and Dean Martin. The 'De Guella' associated with the Mexicans who in 1836 wrested the fortress known as the Alamo from the Texans, was actually written not for the film *The Alamo* (although of course it reappears in it) but for *Rio Bravo*, in which that particular episode in Texan history is made symbolic of Dude's (Dean Martin) struggle against alcoholism. As later in *The Alamo*, 'De Guella' forms the thematic basis of much of the score. Critic John Belton has contrasted the 'epic expansiveness' of *Red River* with

Scene from The Alamo

the 'lyric density' of *Rio Bravo*, and this contrast is reflect in the character of the music. As in *High Noon* Tiomkin relinquishes the *tutti* of the conventional symphony orchestra but this time in favour of the more exotic, specifically Mexican sonorities of marimbas and guitars reinforced by domras and harpsichord, harmonicas, and plucked rather than bowed lower strings which include the 'guitaron', the Mexican bass guitar (no violins or violas). The result is a score of almost chamber-music-like character, much of it nocturnal and atmospheric.

At the London premiere of The Alamo, *October 1960: Tiomkin with Mr and Mrs John Wayne.*

The film drifts in and out *pianissimo* (again like *High Noon*) to the strains of the simple folksong-like main theme; which in the end-title sequence Dean Martin marries to Paul Francis Webster's lyric with its hauntingly repeated last line ('While the rollin' Rio Bravo* flows along').

The Alamo was Tiomkin's last great Western score and an apotheosis of his achievements in this genre. Once again we find the composer responding with forthrightness and intensity to a crucial event in the early history not of his own country — as might have been expected of such a passionate and committed nationalist — but of the land where he had rebuilt his life after its foundations had been destroyed. By chronicling this landmark in Texan history in music of such vitality and fervour, Tiomkin repays his debt to his adopted country with interest. The score ranks with *The Fall of the Roman Empire* as one of the finest of his historical tableaux. *The Alamo* is a cornucopia of Americana *à la* Tiomkin. Its thematic protagonists are the outstandingly popular 'Green Leaves of Summer' (the score's biggest hit-tune); another original Tiomkin composition in folk-ballad style, the 'Ballad of the Alamo'; and the 'De Guella' already mentioned, heard at the outset (Mexican trumpet over a rustling continuum of guitars) in one of Tiomkin's typically understated main-titles. The end-title too is unconventional: 'The Green Leaves of Summer', 'Tennessee Babe' and 'Ballad of the Alamo' set for unaccompanied chorus. 'The Green Leaves of Summer' is employed with laudable discretion in the context of the score itself, while both 'De Guella' and 'Ballad of the Alamo' find their apotheosis in the great battle-sequence which forms the climax of both film and score. Tiomkin does not merely reinforce the noise and tumult of the visual image but adds a dimension, voices the epic, heroic spirit in such a way that we are drawn more positively into the conflict. Particularly effective are the triumphant, ringing proclamations in the *major* of the refrain of the 'Ballad of the Alamo' which stand in marked contrast to the predominantly *minor* tonality of the rest of the music, to the roughly rhythmic thrust of General Santa Ana's theme, and assert the frontiersmen's dogged will to overcome. At the end of the scene the eloquently impassioned 'De Guella' trumpet voices the anguish and despair of defeat and disintegrates amid the debris of bugle-calls and drum-rolls.

*Aside from the river-symbolism implicit in their titles, *Red River* and *Rio Bravo* have this in common: that their heroes' relationships with women are of an incidental, platonic, almost perfunctory nature. In *Rio Bravo* this is reflected in the music inasmuch as Angie Dickinson's slinky saxophone theme stands in marked contrast both texturally, melodically and instrumentally, to all other music in the score.

High Noon (1952)

In his autobiography Tiomkin described the crucial part in the early history of *High Noon* played by the most famous of all his theme-songs, 'Do not forsake me':

> *High Noon* had a preview in a town near Los Angeles. It was a flop... the producers hesitated to release it. It might never reach the theatres... I tried to salvage something... I would see if I could make anything from the song on phonograph records. The record company that handled Tex Ritter (who had sung the song on the soundtrack) wasn't interested, at least not at first. I persuaded another company to issue the song with Frankie Laine. The record was an immediate success, one of the hits of the year... the picture was released four months after, and packed the theatres. The success of the record promoted it. Why had *High Noon* got such an unfavourable reception at the preview? Picture business is full of such puzzles.

Doubtless the fact that *High Noon* was not produced by a major studio but independently by Stanley Kramer and Carl Foreman gave Tiomkin an unprecedently free hand and enabled him to break with Hollywood convention in a number of respects. First: convention decreed that every film should begin and end with a full orchestral *fortissimo*, regardless of its dramatic appropriateness. *High Noon* begins and ends *pianissimo* with a ballad-singer accompanied only by a guitar, accordion and drums. Second: the idea of threading through a single tune, words and all, as an integral part of the dramatic underscore was highly unorthodox; Tiomkin is here anticipating his strategy in the masterly *Gunfight at the OK Corral*. *High Noon*, like *Gunfight*, is virtually monothematic; the tune is the source of practically every bar of the orchestral incidental music, thus ensuring a unique musico-dramatic unity. Third: Hollywood stipulated the use of the standard symphony orchestra in which the main expressive burden fell upon the strings. In *High Noon* Tiomkin dispenses with violin altogether, and the lower strings that remain — violas, cellos and double-basses — are totally subordinated to a wind, brass and piano-dominated sonority. The result is a darker, starker, de-glamorized

Recording the theme song of High Noon *with Tex Ritter* ▷

Sketch for the High Noon *theme song*

quality of tone-colour, one that accords perfectly with the nature of the scenario.

The most elaborate orchestral treatment of the tune occurs at the film's climax: firstly in the montage of suspense which culminates in the arrival of 'High Noon' and with it the 'deadly killer' bent on gunning down Gary Cooper. The clock's ticking is heard first as a throbbing pulse in harp and *pizzicato* strings but grows gradually into a relentless hammering — the whole sequence is in fact a kind of 'fantasia on one note'. Over this *ostinato* the full orchestra throws out a nerve-shattering development of the melodic phrase set in the ballad to the words 'Oh to be torn 'twixt love and duty', the climax being reached with an ear-splitting blast from the whistle of the arriving train. The showdown sequence takes the theme to pieces in an eight-minute-long *tour de force* of variation-cum-symphonic development, and puts it together again, momentously, only in the closing bars as the conflict is resolved.

The Hitchcock Trilogy:
Strangers on a Train (1951), I Confess (1952)
Dial M for Murder (1954)

Tiomkin first worked with Alfred Hitchcock in 1944 on *Shadow of a Doubt* in which the score's main function was to provide a distorted, phantasmagorical version of the *Merry Widow* waltz. (See p.132). *Strangers on a Train* was a more substantial score and Tiomkin's first film for Warner Brothers – the studio for which, in the 1950s, he worked more regularly than for any other.

Hitchcock told François Truffaut that in *Strangers on a Train* he was unhappy with Farley Granger's performance as Guy, the tennis star whom the madman Bruno (Robert Walker) tries to coerce into murdering his father. Ideally Hitchcock would have liked somebody stronger to play Guy's part. This is interesting inasmuch as Guy's theme, and the music that accompanies him throughout the score, is a faithful reflection of the character as he is played by Granger, i.e., somewhat passively and anaemically. Had Hitchcock expressed to Tiomkin his reservations about Granger's performance, composer could certainly have given actor more positive support, could have strengthened him artificially. As for Bruno, Tiomkin always associates his madness with a specific tone-colour as well as with a theme, namely the weird, thin, glassy sound of high violin harmonics. Bruno's theme and Guy's (in a rhythmic, athletic transformation) are alternated to spectacular effect in the famous tennis-match scene, in which Guy has to race against time to finish his game and prevent Bruno planting incriminating evidence in the form of Guy's cigarette-lighter. Here the music not only increases the excitement and suspense but also, as in all scenes where one sequence of events is constantly being intercut with another, supplies much-needed continuity. A similar case is the beginning of the picture, with its alternating shots of the two pairs of legs walking towards each other. It would be premature to differentiate between them musically at this point, and Tiomkin invents a sturdy, cheerful, rather catchy motif for which developments do not permit him to find any further use.

I *Confess* is set in Quebec and concerns a priest (Montgomery Clift) suspected of a murder he did not commit. He knows who the real murderer is because the latter has confessed to him; but, bound by the inviolability of confession, he can make no move to clear himself. The dead man had been blackmailing the priest on account of an affair he had had with a married woman before his ordination, and this explains both the lyrical character of the main theme and Tiomkin's unusual mode of presenting it: we hear it time and again as a soprano solo, but with the sweet, innocent-sounding singer very distantly recorded — so distantly, in fact, that the words are barely distinguishable. The effect is that of a poignant reminder of long-lost happiness. The main-title treatment is particularly poetic. The credits are superimposed on a distant panoramic view of Quebec in silhouette against the evening sky, and the music — *pianissimo sempre* — is literally an illustration of the lyrics:

> While the town is sleeping tight
> Comes the music of the night.
> One can hear its lonely beat
> On each dark deserted street.
>
> The dreams and hopes of yesterday
> Sigh and slowly drift away;
> All the sounds of earth unite
> Secretly in the night.

The magic of the distant solo voice, the velvety, deep-purple key of D flat major (associated with the song throughout the score), the slow, sighing, descending drifts of its melodic profile, the whispered *tenebroso* orchestration — all add up to an evocative tone-picture in miniature,

Rhapsody of Steel *poster*

Search for Paradise *album*

Hitchcock dedication

the intent of which is patently to lull the audience rather than place them on the alert. The shadowy, nocturnal mood is sustained through the opening scene in the darkened church but assumes a quite different character as Clift hears the fatal confession: the unmistakable outline of the *Dies Irae** shapes and repeats itself in the murk with ritualistic *sotto voce* relentlessness. A similar sense of fatalistic implacability lies behind the score's finest dramatic sequence, Clift's decision to give himself up to the police for the crime he did not commit. He walks through the town *en route* for the police station; the picture suggests an image of Christ bearing his cross and the music realizes it in the form of a massive, monumental *marcia funebre*. What we see is Montgomery Clift walking; what we experience, thanks to the music, is both his agony of mind and his integrity, his willingness to sacrifice himself rather than betray his calling: a true *via crucis*.

A later memorable moment when Tiomkin engages our sympathy for Clift follows the courtroom scene; the jury acquits him due to insufficient evidence, but the verdict is unpopular: a hostile crowd in lynching mood surrounds him outside. The starkly passionate music again expresses his bewilderment and that of the real murderer's wife, an unwilling party to her husband's evil. That the latter's mind is giving way during his last confrontation with the priest and the police is subtly insinuated by Tiomkin's use of the soprano saxophone in the accompanying music; another subtlety is the motif for Vilette (the blackmailer/victim) whose unusual (for Tiomkin) 5/4 metre characterizes his nagging, malevolent persistence; this comes as the climax of the long retrospective montage in which Anne Baxter relates to the police the history of her liaison with Clift. Here the music's function, as always in a montage, is that of a binding veneer: it embraces all the diverse elements (young love, dancing in a night-club, the outbreak of war and enforced parting, joyful reunion to the sound of bells in the music, the storm, the encounter with Vilette, the blackmailing), intensifies their momentary significance as they pass, and unifies the entire narrative.

By contrast *Dial M for Murder*, being more or less the equivalent of a filmed stage-play, offered little scope for music. Again in the main title, after a declamatory *tutti* of very brief duration, Tiomkin deliberately disarms his audience by wooing them with a seductive, tuneful salon waltz which plays no part in the ensuing drama. The only sequence in

---

*A favourite of Tiomkin's, as of Rachmaninov's: *Red Light* and *Search for Paradise* are two of the other films in which it appears.

which music really comes into its own is that of the murder itself. Ray Milland plans to have Grace Kelly dispatched by a hired killer while he himself is establishing his alibi at his club. Split-second timing is involved, and Tiomkin responds by turning the orchestra into a monster clock (shades of *High Noon*, although the musical texture and design are quite different, and of Mussorgsky's *Boris Godunov*). He also creates potent atmosphere through the use of dense, bunched chords in the low registers of strings, woodwinds and pianos, played very softly but recorded at an abnormally high level. The cloudy, reverberant sonorities which result are one of the 'fingerprints' of Tiomkin's maturity.

Land of the Pharaohs (1955)

Howard Hawks's *Land of the Pharaohs* was the first of the Tiomkin super-epics; the composer took full advantage of the opportunity here presented him to write on a large and lavish scale. For the most spectacular sequences an orchestra of ninety and a chorus of eighty were employed, the latter under the direction of Jester Hairston. Yet it is typical of Tiomkin's unpredictability that, after an opening flourish of brass, the credits come up to haunting, evocative music, fastidiously scored, whose general dynamic never rises much above a *piano*. A faraway singer rolls back the sands of time five thousand years; in her chant with its strangely primordial, darkly exotic quality are disclosed the two complementary strains of the main theme, both heard above a rustling cimbalom.

The score's biggest set-piece is undoubtedly the music for Pharaoh's procession. The Egyptian legions return in triumph after conquering the Kushites, and the screen explodes in a dazzling spectacle of soldiers, musicians, slaves and spoils. The on-scene instruments are reinforced by a vast ensemble of woodwinds, brass and percussion (bowed strings, being unknown to the Ancients, are omitted: they would anyway impart an undesirable gloss to the sound). The themes — three in all, two from the titles (i.e., the two main themes of the picture) and the theme of the procession itself are not so much developed as engaged in an on-going process of variation. The familiar Russian predilection for oriental colour and glitter is much in evidence, not least in an attractive episode for woodwind and sleighbells. Fanfares of many trumpets announce the arrival of the Pharaoh; the music waxes lyrical and expansive and the sound of girls' voices in the distance is wafted in as on the scents of the most gorgeous flowers. The

With Howard Hawks

scene subsides finally in quiet musings on the main theme as Pharaoh is received by his minister.

The dead of Pharaoh's campaign are honoured in two 'funeral songs of joy' — death for the ancient Egyptians being a cause not so much of sorrow as rejoicing at the thought of rebirth into a new life. Here the chorus becomes not merely an added colour-resource, but an integral, essential part of the musical concept. This is even more true of the film's second big set-piece, the building of Pharaoh's tomb. This is a long montage-like sequence totally dependent on the music to draw it together and urge it onwards; and the voices form a conceptual part of the dramatic substance. Quarrying sounds — hammers and chisels in their thousands — are reinforced by the percussion playing anvils, triangles and steel plates; great blocks of stone are being chipped out of the rock, and Tiomkin embodies the workers' religious zeal and fervour of commitment in two sturdy, chant-like melodies first heard singly, at times in the manner of a chorale, and finally yoked together in counterpoint. The music has a rough-hewn quality, a surging ponderousness of motion, and a spirit which brings to mind works like Mossolov's *Iron Foundry*, Prokofiev's *Age of Steel* and other works of Soviet-inspired, documentary-style realism (an anticipation here too, surely, of Tiomkin's own cartoon documentary *Rhapsody of Steel*).

The themes associated with the Great Pyramid recur later in an eerie, spectral transformation evoking the atmosphere of the subterranean, labyrinthine vaults to which only Pharaoh and Vashtar his architect are supposed to be allowed access. In the climactic scene of the sealing of the tomb, however, the melodic protagonists are the two major themes of the picture; in a spectacular orchestral *tour de force* we hear them chanted by the priests as they wait to be immured in the tomb. The music also intensifies Queen Nellifer's impotent despair as she realizes she is to share their fate; but above all it depicts the rushing and pouring of the great barrages of sand that set the sealing mechanism in motion with an inexorability that no power on earth can stay. The very Tiomkinian racing, scurrying figuration is also used to very different effect in the scene of M'buna's attempt to assassinate Pharaoh, where its intention is patently to conjure up the sound and the feel of the night wind (this bears a strong similarity to the 'Road to Reata' scene in *Giant*, q.v.).

Land of the Pharaohs demanded a certain amount of on-stage or 'source' music, of which the two 'funeral songs of joy' for chorus and orchestra are outstanding examples. A lengthy 'Sudanese dance' consists basically of progressively more elaborate variations on a single, simple

Recording Land of the Pharaohs *on the Warner Bros. sound stage*

theme until a frenzied climax is reached (woodwinds, brass and percussion predominate in the scoring). The thematic material in all these cases is strong, but what is arguably the score's most haunting melody is reserved for Vashtar the architect; its lyrical, intimate character is thrown well into relief by the extrovert grandiloquence of the rest of the score. A lyric by Ned Washington entitled 'This too shall pass' was later written to this melody.

Giant (1955)

Nowhere more strongly do we feel Tiomkin's empathy for Americana and the West than in his score for George Stevens's film of Edna Ferber's Texan epic, a kind of Texas *War and Peace* or *Forsyte Saga*. The main theme, a march, is surely one of the grandest tunes ever written, on screen or off it. Robust and broad-gestured with a tremendous rough-hewn grandeur, it is a musical microcosm of that empire to the West more vast than the minds of urban men can conceive — the empire of Texas 'where the infinite plains and restless cities still beat with the pulse of frontier adventure as did the Chisholm train when the first herds of longhorns thundered eastward to market'. This magisterial melody was later adopted as the Texas State Song. After the massive, sprawling main-title statement it finds its most natural outlet in the scene where Leslie Lynnton (Elizabeth Taylor) is first brought to Reata as a bride by her husband, Bick Benedict (Rock Hudson). They are set down in the midst of a vast, arid, dusty plain, the sun 'burning like a stab wound', the hot unceasing wind giving no relief and blowing wind-rock in all directions. It is from this all-present Texan wind that the music takes its cue. Rags and tatters of the 'Giant' theme, barely recognizable at first, are scattered and borne aloft on a

With George Stevens and Chill Wills on Giant

With Edna Ferber

tireless pitter-patter of strings, playing very softly, very lightly, very quickly. Gradually these dabs and dashes of tune assume coherent shape, broaden, lengthen, louden; until at the climax, as the Reata Ranch heaves into view — a huge edifice of towers and domes and balconies and porticoes and iron fretwork — the 'Giant' theme *in toto* and *fortissimo* is blared forth in bold and brassy splendour.

The love-theme (which later became a popular song under Paul Francis Webster's title 'There'll never be anyone else but you') is a melody which, in one of the early scenes of Bick's courtship of Leslie, underlines in a sudden burst of eloquent lyricism their tacit decision to marry — the starting point of the whole saga. More subtle is its two-edged application in the barbecue scene (where Leslie faints dead away after watching men eating ox's brains straight out of the skulls). Despite her love for Bick, Leslie feels lonely and insecure, cast adrift as she is among foreign people in a strange overbearing landscape. As she wanders around undecidedly, unable to integrate, the love-theme, heard as a single-line melody, no accompanying harmony, no support, reflects her forlornness: the physical constitution of the music is directly symptomatic of the situation it is required to complement. But she is not the only unhappy one present. Lounging in the background is the moody, disconsolate figure of the no-good job boy, Jett Rink (played by James Dean, his last role). We have earlier heard his own theme, given to an accordion; we have also seen that he is strongly attracted to Leslie Benedict. So in this barbecue scene Tiomkin cleverly links Leslie's loneliness with Jett's by playing the love-theme solo, as described above, but on a *solo accordion.* In other words the theme itself stands for Leslie, but the instrument on which it is played involves Jett; and, of course, the theme's overtones as a love-theme automatically invoke something of Jett's inarticulate feelings for Leslie. Little said; much implied.

Jett himself is given a deliberately trivial cowboy theme. Innocuous enough in the early stages on accordion with banjo and guitar accompaniment (when Jett is still the problem child of the ranch) it is inflated to proportions of vulgar monstrousness on heavy brass as the oil derricks start springing up all over the Reata ranchland, bringing him unheard-of wealth and fame. The contrast between the vastness of his riches and the smallness of his mind is tellingly brought out.

Gunfight at the OK Corral (1956)

The music here is handled with the same economy and restraint as characterizes such other Tiomkin scores as *High Noon, Jeopardy* and *36 Hours.* 'The Ballad of the OK Corral' (lyric by Ned Washington) recounts on its own terms the events which led up to the dawning of 26 October 1881, at Tombstone, Arizona, when one of the bloodiest fights in Western history took place. Sung in the original soundtrack by Frankie Laine, it either pre-states the action to come or adds a chanted postscript to what has gone before. Tiomkin's melody has a fine feel and flow to it, one which may be ascribed at least in part to the fact that one phrase grows naturally and organically out of its predecessor — a process not unrelated to the autonomous self-generating nature of folksong, of which Tiomkin's work as a whole bears broad signs. Like *High Noon,* this is an entirely monothematic score: the musical action is all related in some way to the basic material of the ballad.

The extrapolatory process begins almost immediately. The Paramount Seal comes up to a rising-and-falling motif subsequently transformed into the opening phrase of the 'Ballad', which here outlines the basic plot and leads without a break into the scene of Wyatt Earp's (Burt Lancaster) arrival at Fort Griffin. Here the music creates a mood of nervous anticipation but always through gesture and action, however

Piano conductor score (End Title) of Gunfight at the OK Corral

subdued — in Tiomkin the choreographic impulse is never far away (and every phrase of the music is already evolving from the 'Ballad'). No less balletically conceived is the scene when Earp saves Doc Holliday (Kirk Douglas) from a lynch mob whose purposeful menace is enclosed in the rhythm of a slow march. A vituperative climax is reached, the two escape on horseback and Tiomkin effects a neat transition to the next stanza of the 'Ballad' – thus giving shape, rhythm and continuity to the entire sequence of events.

The film's climax arrives when Wyatt's brother is killed by the Clanton gang who terrorize Tombstone, and he, surrendering his badge of office, challenges them to a showdown. Holliday joins the Earps in their stand, and the Clantons are all killed. In this purely orchestral movement Tiomkin varies and develops the ballad material with masterly resource, especially at the moment when the rival factions warily approach each other (*lento sinistramente*); here Tiomkin sets in motion an inexorable *basso ostinato* featuring thick bunched chords in the murky lower reaches of the piano keyboard (a characteristic sound already exploited to great effect in *High Noon*). A moving moment is the coda of this sequence in which the ballad-theme assumes the character of a requiem, with trumpets tolling a knell for the departed. Holliday and Earp ride calmly out of Tombstone; the singer has done with his tale, leaving the orchestra to ring down the curtain in triumph (see musical illustration, pp.106–7).

Rhapsody of Steel (1959)

One of Tiomkin's finest and least-known scores was written for this cartoon documentary produced by the U.S. Steel Company and recorded in Pittsburgh with the Pittsburgh Symphony Orchestra. *Rhapsody of Steel* offers a brief whistle-stop history of steel from the discovery of meteoric iron by primitive man, through the era of structural steel to the Space Age. Now an animated film allows a composer considerably more latitude than a feature, since the music is directly propulsive of the action. The score is prepared prior to the animation and the animators work to the music, and there is no question of calling the composer in after the picture has been shot and cut. So he has much more freedom than usual to develop continuity of line and argument, and in *Rhapsody of Steel* we can hear Tiomkin taking full advantage of it. The subject-matter of the first part — the growth and development of steel through the Iron Age, the discovery of steel in India and its appropriation by the sword-makers of Damascus, finally

Conducting Rhapsody of Steel *with the Pittsburgh Symphony Orchestra*

the birth of the Steel Age in the mid-nineteenth century and modern techniques of processing iron ore and raw materials into steel — allowed free rein to the lyrical dynamism of his characteristic style. There is some affinity too with Prokofiev's 1927 ballet *The Age of Steel* — the same 'steely' singing quality, the same antiseptic exhilaration. It is likely however that Tiomkin evolved his eminently Russian-sounding *style mécanique* independently rather than directly in the wake of such exemplars of Soviet musical 'realism' as Mossolov's *Iron Foundry*. The 'steel' theme is an ascending four-note figure whose simplicity lends itself readily to the typically Tiomkinian, on-going process of repetition-with-variation which holds much sway through the first part (listen for it, for example, enfolded deep in the bosom of the orchestra towards the end of the glimmeringly evocative, dawn-of-time music which immediately precedes the falling of the meteor). Of course the exotic element in Part 1 appealed, and the sinuously seductive veil dance with its langorous melodic charm and colourful ornamentation, is the highlight of a richly evocative sequence.

Part 2, a scherzo, is based on a nonchalant little tune ('I feel

A scene from Rhapsody of Steel

wonderful/for no particular reason') the first phrase of which is merely the first phrase of the steel theme turned upside down. here the animation depicts the part played by steel in a busy, modern urban community, and the music is a playful set of variations on 'I feel wonderful'; a big brassy, jazzily chromium-plated climax is built up in which all the sights and sounds of a seething metropolis seem to converge (among them taxi-horns and police whistles). Its eupeptic spirit is similar to that of the rowdier parts of Gershwin's *An American in Paris,* and perhaps this portion of Tiomkin's score should be dubbed 'A Russian in New York'. The finale mirrors the nobility of man's aspiration to a wider knowledge of the universe in a *fugato* which describes ever-widening circles of movement and energetic endeavour and which, though fraught with a heroic lyricism, is devoid of grandiosity or hollow rhetoric. The astronauts take wing into outer space where meteorites are born; 'perhaps in the not too distant future', concludes the narrator, Gary Merrill, 'man will set about shaping his civilization on earth as carefully as he has shaped the metal that takes him on the greatest journey in all history. The progress of man is the progress of STEEL.' These final moments recapitulate the opening music to form an exultant coda.

Search for Paradise (1957)

Tiomkin had some pertinent remarks to make on the genesis of *Search for Paradise* in the original draft of *Please Don't Hate Me.* Since these were for the most part omitted in the published version I quote them here:

> By the mid-1950s television was harassing Hollywood. Theatre business declined as people stayed home and watched the screen in the living room. Television was a customer for Hollywood movie-making, but that didn't compensate for more than a fraction of the loss. Then at that moment what should appear but a motion-picture medium that packed theatres wherever it was shown, Cinerama. Brought out by newscaster Lowell Thomas, the wide-screen process created such spectacular illusions of actuality that the first production *This is Cinerama* ran on Broadway for two years and was equally successful in one city after another.
>
> Hollywood, astonished, went for wide screen pictures of one sort or another. In theatres everywhere screens broadened out. It became evident also that, with the competition of television, second-rate pictures would slump, and only superior productions would do well

Recording Search for Paradise: *the Himalayas on the cinerama screen*

in the theatres. Mike Todd's *Around the World in Eighty Days* with one species of wide-screen process scored a triumph, for example. I wrote the music for *Giant*, a huge production that scored a first-rate success in the theatres.

Then I got an offer from Cinerama. Lowell Thomas, enthusiast for the remote places of this earth, had brought out *Seven Wonders of the World*, another giant spectacular that was doing well. Now he was following this with a fantasy of the Himalayas, *Search for Paradise*. The Stanley Warner Company, controlling Cinerama, proposed that I write the music for it.

When Tiomkin saw the film with its Himalayan grandeur, old memories came back. *Lost Horizon* with its Shangri-La of Buddhist monks and monasteries had been set in the world of the Himalayas. In filming the Hilton novel Capra and his colleagues had, of course, never been near the Roof of the World. They'd found mountains not so far away. But here were the real Himalayas, and one could sense the ardour that Lowell Thomas and his director Otto Lang felt for the towering solitudes of eternal ice. Tiomkin continued:–

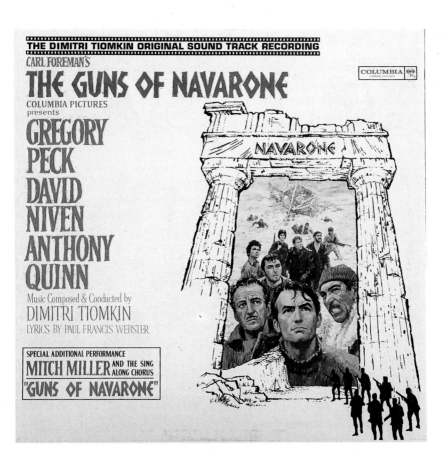

Guns of Navarone *album*

DIMITRI TIOMKIN
IN COLLABORATION WITH MOSFILM STUDIOS
AND MEZHDUNARODNAYA KNIGA
PRESENTS HIGHLIGHTS FROM THE FILM WITH NARRATION BY **LAURENCE HARVEY**

TCHAIKOVSKY

EXECUTIVE PRODUCER **DIMITRI TIOMKIN**
DIRECTED BY **IGOR TALANKIN**
STARRING **INNOKENTI SMOKTUNOVSKY**
AS TCHAIKOVSKY
MUSIC ARRANGED & CONDUCTED BY **DIMITRI TIOMKIN**

Tchaikovsky *album*

Search for Paradise gave me an opportunity to write a score largely of a symphonic character, but in this as an experiment I incorporated songs in the popular style of Himalayan scenes, a lilting ditty for the mountain principality of Hunza, a calypso kind of ballad for the Vale of Kashmir.

Seeing thus in *Search for Paradise** a kinship of spirit to *Lost Horizon*, Tiomkin imbued much of his music for the former with a power of visionary transcendence largely missing in what was in fact, despite its promising title, merely another in the long series of mid-fifties travelogues designed to show off the resources of the tripartite Cinerama screen. Here the Cinerama crew headed by Lowell Thomas stop first in Ceylon for a brief look at local shrines. Then they proceed to the small kingdom of Hunza, where national ceremonies, dances and polo matches are observed. Kashmir, its capital Srinagar and its river boats provide a relaxing interlude before the journey to Nepal and Katmandu, where the coronation ceremony of King Mahendra and its attendant processions are covered in detail. The film ends with a display of American air power, which marks a shift from picturesque tourism to the more sinister world of power politics.

For beauty of sound Tiomkin perhaps never surpassed his *Search for Paradise* score. It functions on two complementary levels: on the one, as a dynamic, pulsating symphony of modern life and landscape; on the other, as a light humorous camera-commentary in sound — hence the songs 'Search for Paradise' (with its Russian falling fourths), 'Happy land of Hunza', the lovely, sweet-scented 'Shalimar Gardens' ('Paradise without Eve'), and the irresistible doggerel calypso 'Kashmir' ('Calypso on Dahl Lake'), all sung by Robert Merrill. But moving and conditioning everything there is what Tiomkin described as a 'sustained theme, now hidden, now prominent — a theme of adventures in sound to faraway places — now the highest reaches of the snow-capped Himalayan mountains, now the languid, flower-perfumed lake of Shalimar; now the foaming torrent of the glacier-fed Indus as it thunders down from the roof of the world'. Evidently the composer was thinking back to the 'theme' (in the broadest general sense) of *Lost Horizon*, but here it happens that a typically Russian *grande envergure* of conception — the 'epic' touch — is unforcedly blended with the fondness for atmospheric effects of colour and light, the dissolving of links of form and colour with the subject via a more

*One of the contributors to the scenario was Prosper Buranelli, co-author of *Please Don't Hate Me* — written, incidentally, at the instigation of Lowell Thomas.

fugitive process of thematic development, that ultimately derives from French Impressionist influence. When Lowell Thomas and company are entertained to tea by the Royal Family 'in a scene reminiscent of a Renoir painting' the picture's theme-tune ('Come ye discontented') is heard in an Impressionistic setting to match. Another conspicuously beautiful example is the 'Deep in Hunza Valley' sequence where a solitary cor anglais sings the virile, upward-striving main theme through a dreamlike haze of muted strings, tubular bells chiming as from a great distance and the chorus singing wordlessly in an evocation of mystic solitudes. A similarly distinguished sequence is 'Indus River'. The Cinerama crew make camp for the night as the setting sun, *molto misterioso*, gilds the 26,000-foot snow-clad summit of Nanga Parbat, known as the killer mountain. The following morning preparations are afoot for a boat-trip – complete with Cinerama Camera – down the treacherous Indus river (bright, brisk *fugato* with donkey-noises from wood blocks [hooves] and braying muted horns). The 'Adventure' theme breaks loose in joyous abandon, natives push the boat out into the stream, and off they go. Tiomkin accentuates this hair-raising episode with an abrasive, aggressive *fugato*. Huge waves hit the boat and splash the camera lens, the shore-line dips crazily up and down, the water becomes rougher and rougher. After a brutally climactic *stretto* there takes place a magical modulation from C minor to major, telling us that the worst of the journey is over; and from now on, *molto calmando*, the music begins to recede into ever remoter regions of enchanted orchestral sonority. As the sun sets over the Indus, and we see the Cinerama crew sitting round a camp fire, their boat silhouetted against the water and sky, the six horns sound the 'Adventure' theme dreamily and distantly and in deep-throated splendour, almost as from beyond the horizon.

The picture opens in the sky near an air base somewhere in the southern part of the United States where they are holding aerial exercises (*allegro impetuoso*). Parachute jumps begin, one after the other (*appassionato*) until the sky is teeming with floating parachutists who one by one touch the ground and disappear. But by now the Cinerama plane is over the water and signals the first full statement of the majestic 'Adventure' theme which acts as a kind of *ritornello*, both during this sequence and throughout the score. Here it is interposed with rolling triplets suggesting the swell of the sea. First landfall after spanning the Atlantic is the monastery of Saint Michel off the northern coast of France ('Dies Irae', the surging sea-triplets persisting in the bass). Now we are once more over terra firma and a panoramic shot

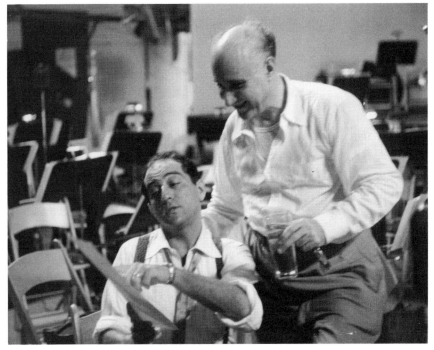

Search for Paradise: *with baritone Robert Merrill*

of the Eiffel Tower dominates the screen (Offenbach paraphrase). The music begins to assume an oriental cast of feature as we fly down the Suez Canal towards Port Said, gateway to the Orient. Along the desolate coast of southern Arabia we pass the port of Mukallah, a port which, says Lowell Thomas, remains unchanged since the days of Sinbad the Sailor; here the music creates an aura of mystery and enchantment before launching into a passionate outburst of lyricism which culminates in a mighty *fortissimo* statement of the 'Adventure' theme. Brief succeeding episodes depict a harbour with small boats and an aerial shot of Bombay — but Cinerama's goal is a region few travellers have ever seen, the principality of Hunza: a valley lying deep between towering peaks at a point where the western Himalayas are flanked by the towering Karakorums.

Mountain solitudes . . . fields of golden wheat and cattle, peasants harvesting. . . . Tiomkin captures the feeling of effortless contentment in a disarmingly simple melody, 'Happy land of Hunza'. A scampering *scherzando* transformation of this tune (with camel bells) depicts a group of native children enjoying themselves in a free-for-all while their elders are engaged in a game of polo, Hunza's national sport.

The picture ends, as it began, in the sky: the Air Force takes us home. We hear the 'Adventure' theme for the last time, and Tiomkin hymns the flight of the four jet planes in vigorous almost neo-Handelian style:

> On silver wings with a spirit that forever sings
> And a disliking for all the ordinary earthly things
> Into far distant sky where the eagle wouldn't try to fly
> On our way to the stars for a close look at Mars
> Off we go!

The jets leave the runway in unison and fly upward and onward into the heavens; soon they are seen as tiny specks in the distance, leaving trails like falling comets:

> Off the ground free are we
> Skyward bound, glory be
> Over land over sea
> We defy gravity, this is our destiny.

The afterburners of the jets light up the night, and the planes are now flying directly into the setting sun which looks like a ball of fire:

> In yonder skies the Aurora Borealis lies....

The planes disappear in the sunset and in the infinity beyond, and the solo baritone brings on the End Title: at this point too Tiomkin performs one of his cleverest contrapuntal sleights-of-hand in combining 'Happy land of Hunza' in the brass with the soloist's 'Somewhere, in the distance....' In the closing bars the chorus aims higher and higher up the scale with their repeated ecstatic cries of 'Search!' and the soloist lands his respondent top G — ('Search for Para*dise*!') — all as if in a concerted effort to reach the stars.

An overture for piano and orchestra (based on what is now known as the theme of *The Old Man and the Sea*, which was originally composed for *Search for Paradise*); evocative music of a delicate oriental stamp for Ceylon and its temples; Himalayan soundscapes; in Hunza, a variety of stylized native dances (including 'Shield Dance', 'Bucephalus Ritual' ['Native Drum Dance'] and a 'Hunza Danza'); a motor-car trip to Katmandu; a rousing march for the Nepal coronation ceremonies and festivities which include a spectacular elephant parade; these complete the quota of highlights for one of Tiomkin's most colourful scores, a gala multi-movement tone-poem, extravagantly and unabashedly programmatic in the best Strauss—Respighi tradition.

Unfortunately the Cinerama phenomenon was short-lived and films like *Search for Paradise* can be screened today only if they are reprocessed for 70mm. The likelihood is, therefore, that future generations will have no opportunity of judging Tiomkin's score in relation to the film. This is not however a major calamity in this case: the music's quality guarantees its survival as an independent entity.

The Old Man and the Sea (1958)

Tiomkin's third award-winning score was for John Sturges's screen adaptation of Hemingway's masterpiece with Spencer Tracy as the Old Man. Here, any objection that Tiomkin's music is too lush for the prevailing plainness and sobriety of Hemingway's prose style can be countered by pointing to the fact that, visually, the film adaptation itself is lush. James Wong Howe's camera seeks out an infinite variety of gorgeous sea- and skyscapes which the composer enhances both in the subtly differentiated balance and shading of his impressionist tone-colours, and in the surge and fall and harmony of his rhythms. The main theme has an immediate lyrical appeal, certainly; but it is also perfectly tailored to Tracey's portrayal of the Old Man's quiet simple dignity and heroism. The melodic formation of its opening phrase is not unlike that of the striving, aspiring 'Faust' theme in Liszt's *Faust Symphony*; and Tiomkin's theme likewise conveys a feeling of ever reaching upwards and on, but in a manner ever serene, ever devoid of bluster and brio. The memorable profile of this theme informs several scenes with the nobility, big-heartedness and undemonstrative grandeur of the Old Man; it also punctuates both the quasi-Cuban folk music in the tavern at Casablanca where the Old Man and a Negro spend two days and nights each trying to force the other's hand down on to the table, and the fight-to-the-death with the great marlin for which the Old Man needs to summon all his strength and powers of endurance. When he makes his first attempt to hook the fish, the music alone is responsible for describing its pull on the line — the camera focuses exclusively on the Old Man's face and we do not see the fish.

The other important motifs are a sunny *scherzando* theme for the Boy (Felipe Pazos), a ruthless, rhythmic tuba theme for the predatory sharks, and a sweet nostalgic melody that survived independently as a song ('I am your dream') for the Old Man as he dreams of the lions playing on the long, golden beaches of Africa. One of the most poetic mood-pictures comes about as a result of an authentic Portuguese fishing-song which Tiomkin himself had collected. In the days before *Lost Horizon*, Frank Capra used to take him for automobile rides

Spencer Tracy in The Old Man and the Sea

along the Californian coast. 'I was filled with wonder at the magnificence of colour and the abstract immensity where ships sailed out to nowhere', he recalls in his autobiography. 'Frank also took me fishing... in the early morning, at sunrise, our boat would put out from harbour amid a swarm of the boats of Portuguese fishermen. There was a Portuguese colony down the coast. Their outboard motors chugged and they sang; it was like a chorus of boats, the sound drifting across the water. Their chant was lilting and lyrical, with a sweetness, yet a darkness, often found in Iberian music.' Years later the memory of Capra's fishing trips and the fishermen's song came back to Tiomkin, and he incorporates it here in the scene of the fishermen's early-morning departure and also briefly in the finale. The deep, dark, distant sound of the men's voices is wonderfully evocative, and in a true Hemingway manner.

The Guns of Navarone (1961)

The setting of this picture – Greece and the Islands of the Aegean Sea at a crucial stage in the Second World War – proved especially congenial to Tiomkin. It is well known that at the time of the break-up of the Roman Empire, Russia inherited not the Latin civilization of the West but the Greek or Byzantine civilization of the East. When in the tenth century priests from the Eastern Empire were brought in to teach Christianity, Byzantine culture began to permeate the Land – the Greek alphabet, literature and liturgical music. Beneath the complex network of Slavonic languages and cultural traditions there thus lies an ancient classical foundation to which it is only natural for a Russian artist to be particularly drawn. Tiomkin was enabled in this way to identify himself more positively than usual with at least the visual aspect of the film. He took the opportunity to steep himself thoroughly in the contemporary folk idioms of the Greek Islands and reproduced them with his customary sureness of touch – in the music for some native wedding celebrations which form a colourful backdrop to scenes of arrest and capture, and in the fashioning of a Greek-sounding melody 'Yassu' ('Farewell') used at intervals throughout the score. The chief musical glory of *The Guns of Navarone* is, however, its splendid main theme, whose two contrasting segments prove themselves capable of all the necessary dramatic development. For instance, it rears itself threateningly in the nether regions of the orchestra in the cliff-climbing scene suggesting both the frightening sheerness of the cliff-face itself and the ever present danger of discovery by the German patrol; and the theme's second strain (see Ex.2) assumes a beleaguered aspect at the moment of the shooting of young Pappadinos. Most important of all (from the musical as well as the dramatic point of view) in the climactic sequence in which the blowing-up of the German guns within the fortress of Navarone before the arrival of the British Navy becomes a desperate race against time. The music's function here is not only to underline the constantly mounting suspense but to thread together the continually changing scenes of focus (the Germans outside the fortress, the saboteurs inside and the Navy ploughing through the Aegean) into a unified dramatic whole. This fine piece of writing takes the form of a free fantasia on the main theme in its essentially heroic aspect, and the familiar strains of 'Rule Britannia' which become increasingly preponderant as the fleet draws closer. At the climactic point the full orchestra falls suddenly away to leave the gentleness of muted strings and a few solo winds musing quietly on the main theme

Composition sketch for the Guns of Navarone *Main Title*

and 'Yassu' elegiacally harmonized; the two parts of the them are even blended harmoniously in counterpoint. Finally Paul Francis Webster's lyrics are heard sung *pianissimo* by the chorus, and as the fishing-boat bearing the survivors of the enterprise sails quietly out of the twilit harbour, 'Yassu' and the faint splashing of the celesta wind this most poetic of Tiomkin's codas to stillness.

The Fall of the Roman Empire (1964)

In *The Fall of the Roman Empire* Tiomkin was no less ideally cast, and produced one of his best – and largest – scores (his orchestra at maximum strength numbered some 130 players). An apotheosis. Russian composers have always been irresistibly drawn to the chronicled history of the early medieval world; tales of heroism and pageantry enacted against a panoramic landscape form the basis of some of the masterpieces of Russian music — Borodin's *Prince Igor*, Mussorgsky's *Boris Godunov* and Prokofiev's music for Eisenstein's *Alexander Nevsky* and *Ivan the Terrible* are cases in point. This is connected partly with an intense historical awareness, partly with an almost child-like preoccupation with colour and with directness and trenchancy of utterance. So Tiomkin's enthusiastic response to Bronston's Roman Empire project was predictable. How was he to interpret his role? He took his cue from the scriptwriters, who had decided to isolate and develop two only of the many factors leading to Rome's downfall — the pressure of barbarians on the frontiers and the tragic reign of the half-insane Commodus. In this way the story-line avoided all trace of diffuseness and allowed scope for the development of plot and character on the purely dramatic plane; and it was this which determined the nature of Tiomkin's approach. He began to feel a degree of personal involvement with the *dramatis personae*:

> ...I decided I must dismiss all idea of giving this picture quasi-documentary-style music. My plan was to react spontaneously to the dramatic element which I gradually began to appreciate in *Roman Empire*. I excitedly started to block important dramatic and lyrical passages and found myself, to my great surprise, involved not with characters from eighteen centuries ago but with characters whose problems were remarkably like our own and practically co-incidental with all human drama. They were amazingly alive, close to me... and then the melodies started to come.,

The musical symbolism in *The Fall of the Roman Empire* is quite intricately worked. The main theme — shared between organ and orchestra during the credits — is gravely beautiful but heavily imbued with a characteristically Slav melancholy; it sets the tone and temper of the entire film, for in addition to symbolizing the downfall of Rome it is also used, in a poignant chromatic harmonization for strings, to underscore the sundering of relations between Lucilla (Sophia Loren), daughter of Marcus Aurelius, and Livius (Stephen Boyd), thus neatly dovetailing the element of personal tragedy with the broader issue of nationwide catastrophe.

Another use of this theme later in the film offers an excellent illustration of the way in which music may invest a scene with an added dimension of meaning, conditioning the audience's reactions in such a way that they become subconsciously aware of the shift in emphasis. This happens in the scene towards the end where the entire population of Rome seems to be dancing a primitive version of the twist. This is accompanied musically by a tarantella, a fast Italian dance with alternating major- and minor-key sections. However, as the orgiastic climax approaches, the tragic main theme suddenly stalks in, spectre-like, first on the organ pedals and then throughout the main body of the orchestra but retaining the garrulous tarantella rhythm as counterpoint. The sudden irruption of this theme in this way thrills with the sense of approaching doom and charges the whole sequence with an undercurrent of irony; it lends the frenzied revelry the character of a *danse macabre*, which is exactly what it is — but with the music the point is made much more forcibly.

This main theme, of course, returns (in the full orchestra reinforced by organ) to bring the picture to a close, but the farewell appearance of certain other motifs in these final moments gives a clue to the nature of their symbolic import. First, a reminiscence of the scene in which Marcus Aurelius (Alec Guinness) had received tribute in turn from all the provinces enjoying the Pax Romana – the Roman Peace of orderly government. The music for this scene is cast as a kind of passacaglia – a single melody repeated again and again, remaining essentially unchanged throughout, but subject to perpetually renewing variation in harmony and orchestral texture. This is the exact musical counterpart of the action on the screen – the representatives of the various provinces may be diversely costumed, but they are united in motive by their pledge of fealty to Aurelius. The appearance of the fine 'passacaglia' theme in the closing stages of the film is subtly ironic, since the undermining of the Pax Romana is already well in evidence, and with it a foreshadowing of the eventual disintegration of the whole Empire.

Panoramic view of a Fall of the Roman Empire *recording session*

The Fall of the Roman Empire — *making a take*

Another pointedly symbolic interpolation before the final uncompromising statement of the 'Fall of Rome' theme is that of a reference to the funeral procession of Marcus Aurelius; but the symbolism of the theme which plays the largest part in this final scene is less obvious. It is a simple folksong-like melody which earlier had provided a mutedly elegiac background to shots of the havoc wrought by invading barbarians, the blackened smoking ruins of villages left in their wake. The final shot in the film is that of a massive conflagration in the Roman Forum, with clouds of billowing black smoke obscuring all from view. The two scenes are linked by the appearance of this theme, now more expressively scored and fully harmonized; it prefigures the ultimate fate of the Eternal City itself at the hands of the approaching marauders (see Ex.1, p.67).

The audience of course may not consciously appreciate this network of cross-references, nor is it to be expected that they should. How they react subconsciously is another matter; it is obvious that when music is used as intelligently and meaningfully as here it cannot but sharpen their receptivity, while at the same time contributing to a rounder and more satisfying synthesis of all the diverse elements of which the film is compound. Yet the score for this picture offers at least one instance of a peculiar dilemma in which most film composers find themselves at one time or another.

For there are times when the composer will want to throw all the cinematographic paraphernalia overboard and allow free rein to his inspiration; a particular incident or situation having fired his imagination, he longs for once to be the sole possessor of his musical material, to nurture and develop it in his own way without constant reference to the extra-musical exigencies of the stopwatch. Tiomkin was acutely aware of this problem when working on *Roman Empire*:

> ... naturally I would have preferred to write music before *Roman Empire* was made and ask the producer to film a picture round it but, alas, the picture was already complete... in the beginning I had a strange desire to develop my themes in a more complex and interesting manner, and when it was time to put the music to the film, with stopwatch, I found myself in conflict with myself.

This is particularly noticeable in the Forum scene where the music runs continuously for some six minutes. Up to the last few seconds the music exists both as a suitable complement to the visual images and as an excellent musical composition in its own right. It is in fact organized along sonata-rondo lines with two basic themes, the periodic recurrence of which is separated by free variation and development in the traditional symphonic manner. These two contrasting themes represent a happy coinciding of symphonic manner with cinematic matter, for the first theme depicting the bustle and hum of activity in the Forum is vigorously extrovert and given to the brass, whereas the second is a lyrical, sweeping, Borodin-like melody for high strings which reflects the gleaming white of the temple-crests against an azure sky. All is well until there is an abrupt cut to the interior of the Temple of Jupiter. The music is forced to make an equally abrupt transition and within seconds to drop out altogether; we feel that the flow of the composer's invention has been arbitrarily stemmed, and the effect is almost physically painful. Should Tiomkin have given himself less latitude and devised a less awkward-sounding transition? From the cinematic point of view, yes; from the abstractly musical point of view

On the set of 55 Days at Peking *with director Nicholas Ray*

the temptation is to say no, for if he had we should have been deprived of an excellent stretch of symphonic writing.

55 Days at Peking (1965)

In 55 Days at Peking, Bronston's painstaking reconstruction of the 1900 Boxer Rebellion, Tiomkin succumbed again, as in Lost Horizon and Search for Paradise, to the lure of the exotic East — to the glitter and profusion of colour, the opulence of the settings and costumes, and that paradoxical melange of barbarism and refinement characterisic of Tartar domination. The typical present-day Russian has, after all, a measure of the Tartar in his own make-up.

The opening bars of the overture (played in the theatre before the picture begins) unleash a tumult of orchestral colour, a firework display, which throws up first of all a splendidly barbaric motif, all spit and crackle and oriental fizz. There follows a sentimental salon air (later a waltz) designed to evoke the rather faded plushness of a turn-of-the-century Embassy hotel; and then the wistful theme song of the picture, 'So little time', in full orchestral dress. By the time it is done the overture has presented all the main themes of the picture except one, and this, the fourth, is a beautiful melody for divided strings which in the main title matches the serenity of the Don Kingman paintings on which the credits are superimposed. This theme is nowhere more movingly employed than in one of the opening sequences where Teresa (Lynne Sue Moon), the little Chinese daughter of Captain Andy Marshall (Jerome Thor), in quest of her father pushes her way anxiously through the crowd cheering the incoming marines. At the beginning of the scene interest centres exclusively round the marching troops, and 'Semper Fideles' and 'Yankee Doodle' are heard in the brass. As the anxious face appears, on the strings the lyrical theme is driven in contrapuntal harness with the march. As we become more and more involved with Teresa's desperate efforst to break through, the string theme surges more and more to the fore and is developed with increasing poignancy, until with a sudden change of focus to the parade it is dismissed and the band re-engaged – an ingenious interweaving of 'on-scene' and dramatic music which enhances the emotional impact of the scene. A composer may often be faced by a scene which badly needs dramatic music but which also has to have on-scene music going on at the same time. Rarely is it possible to combine the two types in viable, euphonious counterpoint, as Tiomkin does here.

Tchaikovsky (1970)

Some felt that Ken Russell in *The Music Lovers* had used Tchaikovsky's life story merely as a peg on which to hang a bizarrely distempered fantasy on homosexuality and nymphomania. Dimitri Tiomkin's *Tchaikovsky* should serve to restore their faith in the ability of the cinema to tell the story of a great artist's life and work without allowing it to degenerate into a morbid catalogue of neuroses, complexes and phobias, many of them exaggerated and fictionalized out of all recognition. *Tchaikovsky* is the exact antithesis of *The Music Lovers*. In its overall pattern and shape it has some affinity with the 'biopics' — film biographies of eminent figures in all walks of life as they were produced regularly in Hollywood from the late 1930s on — but it avoids altogether the besetting faults of these productions: their frequent lapses into cliché and bathos, and their ruinous sentimentality. In texture and idiom the picture maintains a distinctive clarity and freshness of perspective which enables it to make its points convincingly yet dispassionately. It disdains the sledgehammer tactics of a Russell in favour of a more or less continuously factual narrative illustrated, as it were, by the enactment of those scenes which influenced critically the course of the composer's career — in other words it is a classic example of the typically Russian technique of cumulative episodes, the 'series of peep-show slides' (as Prince D. S. Mirsky once described *War and Peace*). Where by way of contrast fantasy is interpolated (one such instance will be described below) director Igor Talankin takes care not to let his imagination run extravagantly riot *à la* Russell.

Emphasis is placed on two cardinally important relationships, one professional, the other personal. Tchaikovsky's association with Nikolay Rubenstein, director of the Moscow Conservatoire, was fraught with innumerable misunderstandings and clashes of temperament; yet it was Rubenstein who, in the composer's lifetime, was probably the most ardent propagandist of his works. The famous Christmas Eve quarrel between the two men is strikingly enacted, with Rubenstein thundering forth the *Emperor* in one room as an example to the delinquent composer of how piano music *ought* to be written, and Tchaikovsky in the adjoining room launching into an equally ferocious assault on his own concerto in agonized protest at his colleague's conservatism — one musical epoch waging warfare upon another. Later Rubenstein is shown as one of the concerto's most enthusiastic exponents, gently reproving a student for condemning as unpianistic the very passage which he himself had singled out for criticism so many years before.

The growing intimacy and final rupture with Nadezhda von Meck is portrayed in the emotional crisis central to Tchaikovsky's whole existence. Here the character of the composer's benefactress is handled with sensitivity and discretion. Points tend to be made in terms of image rather than dialogue. For instance, after she receives her first letter from Tchaikovsky she goes out riding, and we see her whipping on her horse, obviously in a delirium of ecstasy; and after she has received the fateful letter in which the composer announces his intention to dedicate the Fourth Symphony to her and, almost within parentheses, informs her of his marriage to Antonina Milyukova which has just taken place, Nadezhda Filaretovna appears not to react at all; she merely strides into the house from the garden, and one of her sinister black dogs joins the other. This cannily telling detail offsets to perfection the mental turmoil she is experiencing, and not a word has been uttered. The climax and watershed of the liaison is marked by a firework display which she invites Peter Ilych to attend in person; the composer, horror-stricken, flees the estate and we see the von Meck family looking on silently at the celebration, a significantly empty seat beside a grim and white-faced Nadezhda Filaretovna.

The picture was made in Russia by Russian technicians and with an all-Russian cast, and its chief glories are twofold — an outstanding performance by Innokenti Smoktunovsky (a highly acclaimed Hamlet in the Russian film version) in the title-role, and the beauties of Margarita Pilikhina's colour photography. Smoktunovsky makes of the composer a shy, nervous, unassertive individual desperately seeking to regain the emotional equilibrium which his mother's death when he was still a schoolboy has seriously disturbed. In Desirée Artôt he finds something of a kindred spirit, but Rubenstein's interference successfully shatters his hopes in this direction. His marriage to the vulgar and pretentious Antonina Milyukova proves unmitigated disaster; Madame von Meck offers him financial and a peculiarly indefinable kind of emotional stability, but when he finds or thinks he finds himself being drawn into a net he scuttles away like a frightened rabbit. Throughout all these scenes — and some of them are harrowing enough, not least the distracted composer's suicide bid in the River Moskva — it is Smoktunovsky's resourcefulness in not overplaying his part which leaves the most profound impression. His Tchaikovsky is no tempest-tossed hysteric, striving frenetically to weld the splintered fragments of his psyche together against the most impossible of odds. There is no element of caricature or stereotype in his portrayal. This Tchaikovsky is essentially a simple man, one who endures the 'slings and arrows of outrageous fortune' with an outwardly stoical demeanour; only at moments of supreme stress — as in the wedding celebration scene — does he lose his self-control entirely.

Smoktunovsky is well supported by Antonia Shuranova as Madame von Meck; by Eugene Leonov as his valet, a clumsy but good-natured, well-meaning and thoroughly lovable oaf: by Eugene Eustigniev as a cynical and slightly sinister Herman Laroche, and by Vladislav Strzeltchik as Rubenstein — abrasive, outspoken, self-important but fundamentally sincere and devoted to Tchaikovsky, both as man and artist.

Pictorially this is a beautiful film. English viewers will be particularly impressed by some breathtaking shots of the Senate House and King's College Chapel, Cambridge (presumably taken from the tower of St Mary's Church) where Tchaikovsky in company with Saint-Saëns is being awarded an honorary doctorate, cheered on through the railings by hordes of enthusiastic undergraduates (present-day students acted as 'extras' here). Montmartre and the Seine in the rain are attractively limned, but it is the scenes actually filmed on location in Russia which are the most powerful in *Stimmung*-an ice-bound St Petersburg with ice breaking up on the Neva, the cathedrals and cupolas of the Kremlin glinting and shimmering through a haze of winter sunlight, the Moskva, deserted, by night, autumn in Moscow with its gas-lamps and smouldering street-fires, the crisp nut-clean freshness of an early morning in the heart of the Ukrainian countryside, a tremendous panning shot right to the top of a silver birchwood. The colours are pastel-toned, in vivid contrast to the glaring reds and screaming yellows of the Russell film, and the photography points and enhances the narrative without ever degenerating into travelogue prettiness.

Musically it is instructive again to compare Tiomkin's approach with that of Ken Russell, who puts Tchaikovsky's music on to the soundtrack in basically its original format throughout, the actual substance of the music being in no way tampered with. In Tiomkin's film there *are* a number of instances in which Tchaikovsky's music is employed *in statu quo* — for example, the dramatic development section of the *Pathétique* Symphony accompanies the suicide sequence, and the march-like third movement from the same work follows the composer's triumphant progress through Europe and America as conductor of his own works. But elsewhere Tiomkin gave himself *carte blanche* freely to adapt and refashion Tchaikovsky's compositions in his own way, the idea being to fuse it more closely with the action and to achieve a rounder and more unified cinematic whole. In this way he was enabled to make many a salient point on the soundtrack which would have been impracticable had he observed the letter as well as the spirit of Tchaikovsky's music; and because of the natural congruence between his musical language and that of Tchaikovsky, all trace of stylistic disparity was skilfully eradicated.

The Russians did not seek to provide a straight biography, rather a series of related impressions showing something of the composer's lifelong quest for artistic truth and the price in emotional terms he had to pay for it — the type of episodic structure beloved of the Russian creative mind. It is something of an over-simplification to claim that Tiomkin makes his film fit the facts whereas Russell makes the facts fit his film; but at least we can see that while Russell's frequent flights into fantasy made it comparatively easy for him to adapt himself to Tchaikovsky music-wise, Tiomkin, more hidebound by sober fact, found it necessary to adapt Tchaikovsky to him.

The opening scenes depict the composer's childhood, his obsessive love for music and for his mother. As he comes down on tiptoe at dead of night to try the piano he is accompanied by the frosty glitter of celesta, piano and strings playing 'Harvest Song' (from the piano suite *The Seasons*). When little Petya finds the piano locked he turns and looks out of the window; the winter garden seems suddenly to become alive, and music wells up inside him with such force that he turns and flees in terror, holding his hands to his ears. At this point the 'Harvest Song' is shockingly maimed and disfigured by muted brass. Mother arrives, and her theme is taken from the central section of the 'Harvest Song', given to a tender solo violin, and this music is developed to an anguished climax as the coachman brandishes his whip to set in motion the carriage which separates Petya from his mother for the first time. In the form of what was originally a piano miniature, Tiomkin cuts out the heart of one of the major tragedies of the composer's life. There is, of course, no direct musical symbolism here; the music has no special relevance to the action except that it is by Tchaikovsky. But there are many instances where the point of a musical passage would be missed were the audience not able to pinpoint the particular Tchaikovsky theme or segment diverted by Tiomkin to his own purposeful effect (there would be little likelihood of this with a Russian audience which knows its Tchaikovsky). For instance at the beginning of the second part we see that Tchaikovsky's marriage has proved a charade, and he has taken to drinking heavily. He is with his valet Alyosha outside a tavern and at the mention of his wife. Antonina Milyukova, flares up in bitter resentment. The music is based on

Lenski's poignant aria from *Eugene Onegin* (Act II, scene ii, where Lenski laments the passing of his youth and happiness); here, of course, it is developed instrumentally. So too in the earlier scene where, upon receiving his first letter from Antonina in which she professes her unbounded love for him, Tchaikovsky is determined not to act with the heartlessness of Onegin in his opera – which he happens to be writing at the time – and goes to see her. With subtle irony the music is adapted not from Tatiana's famous Letter Scene as we might reasonably expect, but from Onegin's aria in Act I, scene iii, in which he explains to Tatiana that he is temperamentally unsuited to the married state. The glorious melody is first sung by the cellos and violas and later by a solo violin. The irony may be rather abstruse, perhaps even for a Russian audience, but none the less the point is made, and cleverly.

There are numerous other instances. When the composer, restless and unable to sleep, asks Alyosha to tell him the story of *Eugene Onegin*, the music of Lenski's aria in Act I, scene i, ('How happy, how pleased I am at last to see you') begins to germinate in his mind; and this is what we hear as Alyosha speaks, with the vocal part assigned to strings. After the fatal marriage, Tchaikovsky allows himself to be talked into giving a dinner party to introduce his wife to his colleagues, and at one point the waltz from Act II of *Eugene Onegin* is being played on the piano, realistically. As the climax of the festivities approaches, Tchaikovsky, filled with loathing for his wife, herself sick with fear for the future, and his nerves torn to tatters by the farcical irony of the celebrations, eventually loses his self-control and bursts into hysterical laughter. He is a man on the brink of insanity, and the orchestra, taking over the waltz from the piano, mauls and distorts it beyond recognition, turning it into a sort of nightmarish *danse macabre*. (This is interestingly reminiscent of Hitchcock's 1944 *Shadow of a Doubt*, in which film Joseph Cotten plays a homicidal maniac with a penchant for wealthy widows; for the titles, therefore, Tiomkin produced a kind of nightmare version of the *Merry Widow* waltz, decking it out with what he appropriately described as 'horror harmonies and orchestration'.) Later as Tchaikovsky and Turgenev walk along the banks of the Seine after Nikolay Rubenstein's funeral in a Paris chapel, a street band complete with accordion, big drum and cymbals plays a rollicking melody which, on closer inspection, turns out to be none other than the little French chansonette 'Il faut s'amuser, danser et rire' which somehow found its way into the First Piano Concerto's slow movement. Finally, as Tchaikovsky with a sick heart makes good his early-morning escape from Nadezhda von Meck's estate in order to avoid the firework party his patroness had planned in his honour, the melancholy oboe theme from the second movement of the Fourth Symphony – *her* Symphony – is given to a solo accordian over a rustle of balalaikas, a doleful and authentically Russian sound.

On two occasions the picture departs from straight story-telling into fantasy, and the first of these inspires what is intrinsically the finest musical sequence of all. In a recital at the Bolshoi Tchaikovsky hears Désirée Artôt, for him the symbol of an unattainable ideal, sing one of his songs, 'At the Ball'; as she does so he is lost in reverie. He is at an actual ball at the Bolshoi, pushing his way through a bevy of masked dancers in an attempt to reach Désirée. The music is compounded of various waltz segments – 'At the Ball', the third movement from the Fifth Symphony, 'December' from *The Seasons* again – and – a nice touch – capped by a vivid coloratura soprano (unseen) which seems to be beckoning Tchaikovsky on, siren-like. In the manner of Ravel's *La Valse* all are whipped up to a big, lustrously scored climax with harp *glissandi* and bells shooting flaming shafts of light through the orchestra. The intention is to mirror both the increasing animation of the dance and Tchaikovsky's increasingly distraught state of mind. At one point. there is a quite unconsious quotation from the 'ecstasy' motif in *Duel in the Sun;* composers often repeat themselves in this way under the stress of similar emotions.

The scene changes to the open country (though there is no break in the music) and Désirée is speeding along in her troika with Tchaikovsky is hot pursuit in his; but however savagely the driver whips on the horses he seems to come no nearer to overtaking her. The coloratura and waltz-madness erupt into a powerful coda based on yet another piece from *The Seasons*, appropriately called 'Troika'.

So we can see that there is always sound musico-dramatic justification for Tiomkin's Tchaikovsky paraphrases. He does not merely put a superfluous gloss on Tchaikovsky or glamorize his music, but thinks himself into the composer's emotional sound-world, always sympathetically and with poetic relevance to the matter in hand — which is, after all, the telling of Tchaikovsky's own story.

Tiomkin, I feel, regarded his *Tchaikovsky* as a gesture of homage to a spiritual predecessor whose music has been a constant and avowed source of inspiration to all Russian composeers. Tiomkin came from Russia and to Russia, in this picture, he returned both literally and figuratively. *Tchaikovsky* sets a fitting seal on a life spent in the service and practice of music in the cinema.

Principal Awards and Honours

Citation from the US War Department for distinguished service as musical director for scoring and conducting all orientation and training films for Signal Corps, United States Army, World War II.

Chevalier of the French Legion of Honour

Officier of the French Legion of Honour

Chevalier de l'Ordre des Arts et des Lettres

Cruz de Caballero de la Orden de Isabel la Catolica (of Spain)

Honorary Doctor of Law, St Mary's University, San Antonio, Texas

Honorary Citizen of Texas

Plaque S.A.C.E.M.

Western Heritage Wrangler Trustee Award, National Cowboy Hall of Fame and Western Heritage Centre, for outstanding contribution to Western Motion Pictures

Golden Record from Dot Records for 'Thee I love'

National Academy of Recording Arts and Sciences Nominations:-
1961   For Best Instrumental Theme or Song — *The Guns of Navarone*
1961   For Best Sound Track Album or Recording of Score from Motion Picture or Television — *The Guns of Navarone*

Academy of Motion Picture Arts and Sciences Awards:
OSCARS:
1952   Score —   *High Noon*
1952   Song —   'Do not forsake me' (*High Noon*)
1954   Score —   *The High and The Mighty*
1958   Score —   *The Old Man and the Sea*

Nominations:

1940	Score —	*Mr Smith Goes to Washington*
1942	Score —	*The Corsican Brothers*
1943	Score —	*The Moon and Sixpence*
1949	Score —	*Champion*
1952	Score —	*High Noon*
1952	Song —	'Do not forsake me' (*High Noon*)
1954	Score —	*The High and the Mighty*
1956	Score —	*Giant*
1956	Song —	'Thee I love' (*Friendly Persuasion*)
1957	Song —	'Wild is the Wind'
1958	Score —	*The Old Man and the Sea*
1959	Song —	'Strange are the ways of love' (*The Young Land*)
1960	Score —	*The Alamo*
1960	Song —	'The green leaves of summer' (*The Alamo*)
1961	Score —	*The Guns of Navarone*
1961	Song —	'Town Without Pity'
1963	Score —	*55 Days at Peking*
1963	Song —	'So little time' (*55 Days at Peking*)
1964	Score —	*The Fall of the Roman Empire*
1971	Best Foreign Language Film —	*Tchaikovsky*
1971	Score —	*Tchaikovsky*

Complete Filmography

During the 1920s Dimitri Tiomkin produced a vast quantity of miscellaneous songs, short piano and light orchestral pieces and special material for the Albertina Rasch Dancers. Details of these, and of other non-film works, may be found in the catalogue of the Dimitri Tiomkin Collection in the Archives of Performing Arts Special Collections, Doheny Library, University of Southern California.

1930	Broadway to Hollywood (March of Time) (ballet sequence)	MGM
	Devil May Care (ballet sequence)	MGM
	Lord Byron of Broadway (ballet sequence)	MGM
	Our Blushing Brides (ballet sequence)	MGM
	Roast Beef and Movies (ballet sequence)	MGM
	The Rogue Song (ballet sequence)	MGM
1931	Resurrection	Universal
1933	Alice in Wonderland	Paramount
1935	Naughty Marietta (ballet sequence)	MGM
	The Casino Murder Case	MGM
	Mad Love	MGM
	I Live My Life (If You Love Me)	MGM
1937	Lost Horizon	Columbia
	The Road Back	Universal
1938	Spawn of the North	Paramount
	You Can't Take it With You	Columbia
	The Great Waltz	MGM
1939	Only Angels Have Wings	Columbia
	Mr Smith Goes to Washington	Columbia
	Daredevils of the Red Circle (12-chapter serial)	Republic

1940	Lucky Partners	RKO
	The Westerner	United Artists
1941	Meet John Doe	Warners
	Forced Landing	Paramount
	Scattergood Meets Broadway	RKO
	Flying Blind	Paramount
	The Corsican Brothers	United Artists

Scores for wartime documentaries
1942 — 1945

	The Nazis Strike	U.S. War Dept. (Later Army Pictorial Service)
	Divide and Conquer	
	The Battle of Britain	
	The Battle of Russia	
	The Battle of China	
	War Comes to America	
	Know Your Enemy — Germany	
	Know Your Enemy — Japan	
	Know Your Enemy — Britain	
	The Battle of San Pietro	
	The Negro Soldier	
	Substitution and Conversion	
	Two Down — One to Go	
	Operation Titanic	
	Tunisian Victory (with William Alwyn)	
1942	A Gentleman After Dark (Heliotrope Harry)	United Artists
	Twin Beds	United Artists
	The Moon and Sixpence	United Artists
	Shadow of a Doubt	Universal
1943	The Unknown Guest	Monogram
1944	The Imposter	Universal
	The Bridge of San Luis Rey	United Artists
	Ladies Courageous	Universal
	When Strangers Marry	Monogram

	Forever Yours	Monogram
	Danger Woman	Universal
	Renegades of the Rio Grande	Universal
	Riders of the Santa Fé	Universal
	Sergeant Mike	Columbia
	Master Key (serial)	Universal
1945	Jungle Captive	Universal
	Dillinger	Monogram
	China's Little Devils	Monogram
	Pardon My Past	Columbia
1946	Whistle Stop	United Artists
	Black Beauty	20th Century Fox
	Angel on my Shoulder	United Artists
	The Dark Mirror	Universal
	Duel in the Sun	Selznick
	House of Horrors	Universal
	Strange Conquest	Universal
1947	It's A Wonderful Life	RKO
	The Long Night	RKO
1948	Tarzan and the Mermaids	RKO
	The Dude Goes West	Allied Artists
	So This is New York	United Artists
	Red River	United Artists
1949	Canadian Pacific	20th Century Fox
	Champion	United Artists
	Portrait of Jennie	Selznick
	Home of the Brave	United Artists
	Red Light	United Artists
1959	Dakota Lil	20th Century Fox
	Guilty Bystander	Film Classics
	Champagne for Caesar	United Artists
	Dead on Arrival	United Artists
	The Men	United Artists
	Cyrano de Bergerac	United Artists
	Mr Universe	United Artists
1951	The Thing (GB title: The Thing from Another World)	RKO
	Strangers on a Train	Warners
	Peking Express	Paramount
	The Well	United Artists

	Drums in the Deep South	RKO
	Bugles in the Afternoon	Warners
1952	Mutiny	United Artists
	My Six Convicts	Columbia
	The Lady in the Iron Mask	20th Century Fox
	The Happy Time	Columbia
	The Big Sky	RKO
	High Noon	United Artists
	The Fourposter	Columbia
	The Steel Trap	20th Century Fox
	Angel Face (The Murder)	RKO
1953	Jeopardy	MGM
	I Confess	Warners
	Return to Paradise	United Artists
	Blowing Wild	Warners
	Take the High Ground	MGM
	Cease Fire	Paramount
	Mission Over Korea	Columbia
	Serpent of the Nile	Columbia
1954	His Majesty O'Keefe	Warners
	The Command (Rear Ground)	Warners
	Dial 'M' for Murder	Warners
	The High and the Mighty	Warners
	A Bullet is Waiting	Columbia
	The Adventures of Hajji Baba	20th Century Fox
1955	Strange Lady in Town	Warners
	Land of the Pharaohs	Warners
	The Court Martial of Billy Mitchell	Warners
1956	Friendly Persuasion	Allied Artists
	Tension at Table Rock	RKO
	Giant	Warners
1957	Gunfight at the OK Corral	Paramount
	Night Passage	Universal
	Search for Paradise	Cinerama
	The Young Land	Columbia
1958	Wild is in the Wind	Paramount
	The Old Man and the Sea	Warners
1959	Rio Bravo	Warners
	Last Train from Gun Hill	Paramount
	Rhapsody of Steel	United States Steel

1960	The Unforgiven	United Artists
	The Alamo	United Artists
	The Sundowners	Warners
1961	The Guns of Navarone	Columbia
	Town Without Pity	United Artists
	Last Sunset (theme song only)	Universal
1962	Without Each Other	Allan Klein
1963	55 Days at Peking	Allied Artists
1964	The Fall of the Roman Empire	Paramount
	Circus World (GB title: The Magnificent Showman	Paramount
	Contrapuntal	Paramount
1965	36 Hours	MGM
1967	The War Wagon	Universal
1968	Great Catherine	Warners
1969	Tchaikovsky	D.Tiomkin/ Mosfilm

Index

Abraham, Gerald, 65–6, 68–70
Age of Steel (Prokofiev), 101, 109
Aha!, 41
Alamo, The, 70, 72, 73, 87–91
Albertina Rasch Dancers, 31, 33, 40, 45, 71, 87
Alexander II, Tsar, 19
Alexander Nevsky, 44, 121
'Alexander's Ragtime Band', 22, 49
Alice in Wonderland' 42–3
American in Paris, An, 111
Angel Face, 70, 72
Artôt, Desirée, 129, 133
'At the Ball' (Tchaikovsky), 133

Bakaleinokoff, Mischa, 45
Balakirev, Mily, composer, 68, 70–1
Bariatinsky, Princess, 19–20, 22
Battle of Russia, 45, 49
Baxter, Anne, 98
Baxter, John, 63
Beethoven, Ludwig van, 48, 53, 66
Berlin, 13, 20, 63, 71; Tiomkin in, 27–30
Big Sky, The, 67, 72, 73–4, 87
Blades, James, 47
Blok, Alexander, poet, 25
Blumenfeld, Felix, 14, 33
Boone, Pat, 54
Boris Godunov (Mussorgsky), 66, 99, 121
Borodin, Alexander, 49, 66, 68, 71, 121, 125
Boyd, Stephen, 122
Brahms, Johannes, 53
Brando, Marlon, 71
Broadway theatre, 38, 82, 111; Tiomkin as producer, 41–2
Bronston, Samuel, film producer, 49, 73, 121, 127
Buranelli, Prosper, writer, 113n, 58
Busoni, Feruccio, 28, 31, 33, 40

California, 63, 118; Tiomkin in, 40–58
Canadian Pacific, 67, 74
Capra, Frank, 42–4, 48, 49, 51, 79, 80, 86, 112, 117–18
Carnegie Hall, 35, 38, 42
Carroll, Lewis, 42
Ceylon, 113, 116
Chaliapin, Feodor, 30–1
Champagne for Caesar, 74
Champion, 73, 74
Chevalier, Maurice, actor, 38
Chopin, Frédéric, 20, 31
Cinerama, 111–17
Clift, Montgomery, 88, 96, 98
Coates, Albert, 45
Como, Perry, 53–4
Conservatoire, St Petersburg, 13, 14, 16–20, 22–6, 33, 45, 49
Cooper, Gary, 52, 95
Cotton, Joseph, 86, 132
Court-Martial of Billy Mitchell, The, 55, 72
Cutting Expenses Down, 41
Cyrano de Bergerac, 70, 74

Dargomizky, Alexander, 69
Dean, James, 105
Debussy, Claude, 18–19, 30, 68
Delius, Frederick, 64
Dial M for Murder, 95–9
Dickinson, Angie, 91
D.O.A., 70, 74
Docker, Robert, 47
'Do not forsake me' (*High Noon*), 52, 53, 72, 73
Duel in the Sun, 62, 78, 84–7, 133
Dukas, Paul, 30

Eichheim, Henry, 79–80
Eisenstein, Sergei, 44, 121
Elman, Mischa, 13

Emanuel, Manuel, 72n
Eugene Onegin (Tchaikovsky), 132
Europe, 20, 31, 36, 38, 49, 58, 63, 66, 130

Fall of the Roman Empire, The, 66, 67, 68–9, 70, 91, 121–6
Ferber, Edna, 102
55 Days in Peking, 68, 72–4, 127
Foreman, Carl, 49, 52, 92
Foster, Stephen, 85, 88
Fourposter, The, 73, 74
France, 14, 68, 114; Tiomkin in, 30–1, 36, 38
Friendly Persuasion, 53, 72, 74

Germany, 14, 20, 23, 24, 33, 119; Tiomkin in, 27–30
Gershwin, George, 35, 36, 38, 40, 80, 82, 111
Gest, Morris, 31, 33, 42
Giant, 67, 72, 84, 101, 102–5, 112
Glass, Montague, writer, 41
Glazunov, Alexander, 14, 16–18, 20, 22, 24, 25, 28, 49, 67
Glinka, Míkhail, 67, 68
Gnessin, Mikhail, 14
Gogol, Nikolai, 70
Goldwyn, Sam, 44
Golschmann, Vladimir, 38
Grace of Monaco, Princess, 73, 99
Granger, Farley, actor, 95
Great Waltz, The, 44
Great War *see* World War I
'Green leaves of summer, The' (*The Alamo*), 72, 73, 91
Guinness, Alec, 122
Gunfight at the O.K. Corral, 62, 64, 66, 70, 92, 105–8
Guns of Navarone, 47, 52 67, 68, 72, 73, 119–21

Hairston, Jester, 72n, 78, 88, 99
Hajji Baba, 74, 139
Hall Johnston Choir, 78, 82
Happy Time, The, 74
Harris, Richard ('Dick'), 72n
Hathaway, Henry, 44
Hawks, Howard, 49, 87, 99
Hemingway, Ernest, 117, 118
High and the Mighty, The, 53, 61
High Noon, 52, 64 , 66, 70–3, 89–90, 92–5, 105, 108
Hilton, James, 82, 112
Hitchcock, Alfred, 49, 71, 95–99, 132

Hollywood, 40–2, 44, 48, 49, 51, 57, 58, 61–3, 65, 68, 71, 73, 77, 80, 82, 84, 92, 111, 128
Hollywood Bowl, 45, 82
Hope, Bob, 53
Hudson, Rock, 103

I Confess, 71, 74, 95–99
D'Indy, Vincent, 30
It's a Wonderful Life, 51, 72

Jeopardy, 105
Jones, Jennifer, 85, 86

Khariton, Michael, 29–33
Karsavina, Tamara, 24, 31
Kerensky, Oleg, 24
Kramer, Stanley, 52, 92

Laine, Frankie, 92, 105
Lancaster, Burt, 105
Land of the Pharaohs, 66, 68, 70, 78, 87, 99–102
Lang, Otto, 112
Last Train from Gun Hill, 62
Linder, Max, comedian, 17
Loren, Sophia, 122
Lost Horizon, 43–5, 64–9, 72n, 77–84, 86, 112, 113, 117, 127

Marquardt, Paul, 72n
Mars Ballet, 40–1
Martin, Dean, 88, 90
Mayakovsky, 19, 25
Meck, Nadezhda von, 129, 133
Meet John Doe, 48, 86
Men, The, 71, 74
Merrill, Gary, 111
Merrill, Robert, 113
Meyerhold, 19, 25
Milland, Ray, 99
Mompou, Federico, 40
Moscow, 22, 44, 130
Mossolov, Alexander, 101
Mr Smith Goes to Washington, 67
Music Lovers, The, 128, 130
Mussorgsky, Modest, 18, 49, 66, 69, 71, 83, 99, 121

Nelson, Ricky, 88
New York, 31, 33, 36, 63; Carnegie Hall,

35, 38, 42; Metropolitan Opera House, 30–1
Nicholas II, Tsar, 24
Night Passage, 72

Obolensky, Prince Serge, 22–3, 33, 63
'Ode to Joy' (Beethoven *Ninth Symphony*), 48
Old Man and the Sea, The, 53, 67, 68, 70, 80, 116, 117–18
Only Angels have Wings, 87
Oscar awards, 52–3

Paris, 58, 63, 115, 130, 132; Opéra, 37, 82; Tiomkin in, 30–1, 36, 38–9
Parrish, George, 72n
Patch, Olivia, Tiomkin's second wife, 58
Pathétique symphony (Tchaikovsky), 130
Peck, Gregory, 85
Perry, Alfred, 72
Petri, Egon, 28
Petrograd, 20, 23-5, 27, 28; *see also* St Petersburg
Pittsburgh Symphony Orchestra, 108
Please Don't Hate Me, 65, 78, 80, 111, 113
Portrait of Jennie, 68, 78
Portuguese music, 117–18
Poulenc, Francis, 35
Preminger, Otto, 55, 72
Prince Igor (Borodin), 66, 121
Prince and the Princess Waltz, the, 73
Prokofiev, Sergei, 13, 19, 38, 44, 45, 49, 66, 101, 109, 121

Rachmaninov, Sergei, 31, 45, 98
Rainier of Monaco, Prince, 73
Rasch, Albertina, ballerina and wife of Tiomkin, 31–6, 38, 40–3, 45, 58, 61
Ravel, Maurice, 30, 35, 38, 40, 133
'Rawhide' theme, 72
Red Light, 98
Red River, 62, 70, 87–91
Respighi, Ottorino, 116
Resurrection, 42
Return to Paradise, 72
Rhapsody in Blue (Gershwin), 35, 36, 38
Rhapsody of Steel, 70, 73, 101, 108–11
Rimsky-Korsakov, composer, 18, 49, 53, 67, 68, 70–1
Rio Bravo , 87–91
Ritter, Tex, 53, 92
Rubenstein, Nikolay, 128, 132
Russell, Ken, 128, 130, 131
Russia, 28, 30–1, 35, 41, 45, 49, 57–8, 61, 62, 65, 66, 74, 80, 99, 119, 127, 129, 131;

music in, 68–70, 113, 121, 133; Revolution in, 16, 23–7; Tiomkin's early life in, 13–27

St Petersburg, 13–14, 16–20, 22–6, 28, 33, 45, 49, 63, 71, 130; *see also* Petrograd
Saint-Saëns, Camille, 130
Search for Paradise, 68–9, 70, 72, 108, 111–17, 127
Selznick, David O., 84–5
Shadow of a Doubt, 95, 132
Shostakovich, Dimitri, 16–17, 25, 66
Shuranova, Antonia, 130
Six, Les, 30
Skryabin, Alexander, 25, 86
Smoktunovsky, Innokenti, 129, 130
Spaeth, Dr Sigmund ('Tune Detective'), 53
Spawn of the North, 80
Steel Trap, The, 74
Steiner, Max, 65, 77, 78, 80
Stevens, George, 102
Stokowski, Leopold, 73
Strange Lady in Town, 87
Strangers on a Train, 70, 95–9
Strauss, Johann, 44, 53, 116
Strauss, Richard, 44, 53
Stravinsky, Igor, 65/66
Studies in Russian Music, (Gerald Abraham), 65
Sturges, John, 117
Sundowners, The, 74

Take the High Ground, 74
Talankin, Igor, 128
Tamkin, David, 72n
Tansman, Alexander, 40
Tarzan and the Mermaids, 68, 74
Taylor, Elizabeth, 103
Taylor, Herb, 72n
Tchaikovsky, Peter Ilytch, 49, 65, 74, 128–33
Tchaikovsky, 57–8, 128–33
Tension at Table Rock, 72
Texas, 84, 86–88, 91, 102, 103
'Thee I love' (*Friendly Persuasion*), 53, 72
Thing, The, 74, 87
36 Hours, 74, 105
Thomas, Lowell, 112–14
TIOMKIN, Dimitri, biographical entries: to America, 31; and ballet, 24, 35, 40–1; as Broadway producer, 41–2; as concert pianist, 28–33, 36, 38, 40–1, 45; as conductor, 45, 47-8; as film composer, 40–57; as a film director, 57–8; to

Hollywood, 40; marriages, 35, 58;
Oscar awards, 52–3; in Paris, 30-1, 36,
38; in Russia, early life, 13–27, 57–8; in
vaudeville, 31–3, 35; in wartime, 48–9
Todd, Mike, 112
Tolstoy, Leo, 41, 70
Tracy, Spencer, 117

Ukraine, 13–14, 25, 49, 62, 130

Wagner, Richard, 86–7
Warner, H.B., 83
Warner Brothers, 78, 95

Washington, Ned, 72, 102
Wayne, John, 53, 61, 87–91
Webster, Paul Francis, 55–6, 72, 90, 104,
121
Weill, Kurt, 72
Well, The, 74
Welles, Orson, 86
Western films, 62–3, 73, 86, 87, 105
World War I, 17, 20, 23–4
World War II, 48–9, 119
Wyler, William, 49

Young Land, The, 73